Purposeful Evangelism and Missions

Donald K. Stewart (D.Min., D.M.E.)

Purposeful Evangelism and Missions
Missing Dimensions

Outskirts Press, Inc.
Denver, Colorado

The opinions expressed in this manuscript are solely the opinions of the author and do not represent the opinions or thoughts of the publisher. The author has represented and warranted full ownership and/or legal right to publish all the materials in this book.

Purposeful Evangelism and Missions
Missing Dimensions
All Rights Reserved.
Copyright © 2010 Donald K. Stewart (D.Min., D.M.E.)
v2.0

Cover Photo © 2010 JupiterImages Corporation. All rights reserved - used with permission.

This book may not be reproduced, transmitted, or stored in whole or in part by any means, including graphic, electronic, or mechanical without the express written consent of the publisher except in the case of brief quotations embodied in critical articles and reviews.

Outskirts Press, Inc.
http://www.outskirtspress.com

ISBN: 978-1-4327-5718-2

Outskirts Press and the "OP" logo are trademarks belonging to Outskirts Press, Inc.

PRINTED IN THE UNITED STATES OF AMERICA

Contents

Foreword i
Preface iii
Dedication v
Introduction vii
Chapter 1: God's Heart For World Evangelization 1
Chapter 2: From Every Tribe, Language, People, Nation 5
Chapter 3: And This Gospel of The Kingdom 11
Chapter 4: Through Jesus Christ Alone 17
Chapter 5: But The Workers Are Few 25
Chapter 6: Empowered To Be Witnesses 35
Chapter 7: And These Signs Shall Accompany 43
Chapter 8: While You Are Going 51
Chapter 9: All Things To All Men 59
Chapter 10: Culture, Customs and Concerns 67
Conclusion 77
Appendix 1 85
Appendix 2 93
Appendix 3 101

FOREWORD

The lessons presented in this text are the outcome of research and hard work on the part of the presenter, Dr. Donald Stewart. He has, in addition, used his own Sunday morning classes (Discipleship Seminars) at Portmore Lane Covenant Church as a means of fine tuning the material to make it as beneficial as possible.

At a time when many Bible Scholars and Church Leaders find it expedient not to embrace the Scriptures as the unadulterated Word of God, the author shows a willingness to be *a voice in the wilderness* in his uncompromising alignment and allegiance to biblical truth. He clings unapologetically to the fact that mankind's salvation lies only in Jesus Christ.

In light of this truth, every chapter of this book is undergirded by a heart for missions and compassion for the lost. It is this kind of heart that inspired (for example) the chapter on Culture, which treats with respect the differences among various peoples, while maintaining the universality of the Gospel.

Each chapter deals with an aspect of evangelism in a manner which lends itself to vigorous discussion and invites the participant to carefully examine long-held beliefs. The material is simple without being simplistic, and the truths are presented in a style that is straightforward and easy to follow.

Although each chapter is highly beneficial on its own, the sequence in which the chapters have been presented contributes significantly to the success of the study.

The opening chapter deals with the heart of God for the lost, and succeeding chapters develop on the believer's role and function in fulfilling God's desire for the world.

The Scripture verses which accompany each chapter provide an opportunity for a disciplined and structured immersion in the Word, as one seeks to verify the accuracy of what is presented.

Those who have had the opportunity to engage with the material in a teacher- facilitated class setting have been informed, challenged, inspired and motivated to pursue a lifestyle of soul winning. The optimum benefits of the study are likely to be achieved in a setting where participants feel free to voice questions, doubts, opinions and suggestions.

Having benefitted so tremendously from these studies, as a part of the Sunday morning classes, it is my prayer that many groups of believers will be engaged with this text, and that its impact will be felt throughout the Church in Jamaica and beyond.

Patricia Rochester
Educator

PREFACE

This book, "Purposeful Evangelism and Missions: Missing Dimensions", was developed in December 2009 as a product of the Sunday morning Discipleship Seminars conducted at the Portmore Lane Covenant Community Church (Jamaica W.I.), from September to November 2009.

In addition to the Introduction and Conclusion, it comprises 10 Chapters which correspond to the 10 Sessions in this Module, as outlined in the accompanying Workbook.

Purposeful Evangelism and Missions: Missing Dimensions is designed to be read independently for personal development or to be used as a Text, alongside the Workbook, in a structured teacher-led class environment.

A *Test and Answer Booklet* is also available to complete the package.

Each chapter is a discussion of Bible-based principles that relate to the Christian's evangelism/missions mandate, with an emphasis on the application of these truths to our daily lives.

The student is encouraged to approach these chapters with honesty, child-like faith and openness for change.

It is important to check and read the given Scripture references, and take the time to meditate on the biblical principles, concepts and instructions, as you complete the blanks in the Workbook.

It is our hope that this Text, along with the Workbook, will provide critical insights, vital understanding and the necessary motivation for countless sincere Christians who normally feel like a *fish out of water*, when previously attempting to evangelize.

Purposeful Evangelism and Missions has been written to provide motivation for further studies in World Evangelization, and in helping Christians to mentor (disciple) others in becoming authentic lifestyle evangelists.

Special appreciation is being expressed to the leadership and members of the Portmore Lane Covenant Community Church who served as willing *guinea pigs* in the processing and development of this, and the other seminar series. My sincere gratitude also to Sharon Knight who took on the tedious task of editing this material.

Thanks to the ever-present Holy Spirit who continues to provide insight, revelation, inspiration, wisdom, motivation, and the necessary finances, in order to effectively advance the Kingdom of God, through the systematic impartation and propagation of His Word.

It is our hope that as you participate in this course and/or complete this Text, you will better understand God's call on your life to "make disciples of all nations"... while you are going.

We trust that you will also commit yourself to serve as an active part of the trans-cultural rescue mission, in which, as militant soldiers of Jesus Christ, Christians everywhere are engaged in snatching souls out of the fire, restoring the battered and setting the captives free.

Donald K. Stewart
Portmore Lane Covenant Community Church
December 2009

Special Note: All Scripture portions are from the New International Version (N.I.V.), unless otherwise stated.

DEDICATED
TO
THE COMMITTED MEMBERS
AND FRIENDS
OF
THE PORTMORE LANE
COVENANT COMMUNITY CHURCH
IN
JAMAICA

INTRODUCTION

The twenty - first century brings with it a season of secular humanism, moral relativism and religious pluralism.

It is a period in which society encourages each individual to do as he sees fit (based on whatever he conceives to be right in his own eyes) with little or no reference to norms, standards and absolutes.

Truth and morality, it is said, are relative and ever-changing concepts, based on the dictates of situational ethics, social trends and the prevailing world philosophies.

It is within such a context that the Ecumenical Movement with its inter-faith dialogue thrives, while Bible-based evangelism is brushed aside as being intolerant, insensitive, inadequate, inferior, inappropriate and irrelevant.

Each present-day Christian must therefore make the increasingly difficult choice whether to identify with *enlightened cutting edge* ecumenical initiatives or strive for *obsolete, old-fashioned* world evangelization.

We will either flow with the popular trend of conveniently accepting, embracing and affirming every religion as an equal pathway to God, or dare to maintain the old-fashioned belief that Jesus Christ is the one and only way.

There are those, like myself, who hold unswervingly to the uniqueness of Jesus' birth, life, death, burial, resurrection and ascension.

We believe that He is "the way, the truth and the life" (John 14:6), the "one mediator between God and men" (1 Tim. 2:5), and the only "atoning sacrifice for our sins" (1 John 2:2), because as far as we are concerned:

> "Salvation is found in no one else, for there is no other name under heaven given to men by which we must be saved" (Acts 4:12).

Paul, writing in Romans 1:16-17, made it crystal clear that it is through this gospel that God displays His power to save, and imparts His righteousness to all those who believe.

When Paul and Silas were asked, by a trembling jailer; "Sirs, what must I do to be saved?" (Acts 16:30) their immediate response was:

> "Believe in the Lord Jesus and you will be saved – you and your household" (Acts 16:31).

John again reminded us that:

> "God has given us eternal life, and this life is in his Son. He who has the Son has life; he who does not have the Son of God does not have life" (1 John 5:11-12).

The gift of salvation (or eternal life) is received only by those who have consciously and deliberately placed their faith in the finished work of Jesus Christ, the eternal "Lamb of God, who takes away the sin of the world" (John 1:29)", the one who:

> "was chosen before the creation of the world, but was revealed in these last times for your sake" (1 Peter 1:20).

The simple, yet profound truth, revealed in John 1:12 is that:

INTRODUCTION

"to all who received him, to those who believed in his name, he gave the right to become children of God".

It follows, therefore, that all others (those who have not accepted him) are not yet the "children of God".

The Bible does not recognize any such phenomenon as "Anonymous Christians", where people are declared to be saved or affirmed to be Christians, based on their levels of morality, religiosity or spirituality, without their personally accepting Jesus Christ as Savior and Lord.

There is also no place in the Scriptures for the concept of "community salvation", where individuals, particularly little children, are considered to be saved on the basis of "the faith of other people", as is taught in churches which practice "infant baptism".

In the same way that the devout, God-fearing Cornelius (Acts 10), the zealous, religious Saul of Tarsus (Acts 9) and the spiritually thirsty Ethiopian Eunuch (Acts 8:26-40) all needed their personal encounters with Jesus Christ, we too all need to be Born Again.

It really does not matter, from God's perspective, whether you are a teacher of the Law like Nicodemus (John 3), a dealer in purple cloth like Lydia (Acts 16: 13-15), a high-ranking official like the pro-consul Sergius Paulus (Acts 13:6-12) or a violent blasphemer and murderer like Saul (1 Tim. 1:12-16)… the plan of salvation remains the same for all.

This is so, even though countless intellectuals have reasoned away the need for a biblically-based salvation, and the liberal theologians have redefined God's requirements, to exclude concepts such as blood atonement, Christ's substitutionary death, regeneration, repentance and personal faith in Jesus Christ.

The cry still echoes through the centuries:

"We must pay more careful attention, therefore, to what we have heard, so that we do not drift away. For if the message spoken by angels was binding, and every violation and disobedience received its just punishment, how shall we escape if we ignore such a great salvation?" (Heb. 2:1-3)

While the authentic Christian is not authorized to force any human being, anywhere, to personally accept the eternal life that comes through Jesus Christ, we are nevertheless commissioned to proclaim this life-transforming Gospel to the ends of the earth.

World evangelization and missions are not simply abstract, theological concepts or optional activities for the brave, energetic or naïve who have not yet settled on a real career path.

In the midst of all the ecumenical confusion around us, God still expects us to "make disciples of all nations" as we proclaim the Gospel of his Kingdom to all creatures everywhere.

Are you ready for that adventure? The time to prepare is now.

CHAPTER 1

God's Heart For World Evangelization

> "The Lord is not slow in keeping his promise, as some understand slowness. He is patient with you, not wanting anyone to perish, but everyone to come to repentance" (2 Pet. 3:9).

Possibly the most well known verse in the entire Bible is John 3:16. It has been translated into hundreds of different languages and dialects all over the globe, carrying a simple (yet profound) message of God's love for all humanity.

This is a passage, known far and wide, by the saint and sinner alike. Adults of every race, nationality and culture, in all regions of the world where the gospel message has been preached, can easily recite John 3:16, without even pausing for air.

Even the youngest child in your own community, as long as he or she had been exposed to church, Sunday school or family devotions, can articulate with confidence:

> "For God so loved the world that he gave his one and only Son, that whoever believes in him shall not perish but have eternal life" (John 3:16).

It is important to note, however, that though God loves everyone, it is only those who believe in him and who accept the gift of his Son that will have eternal life.

Like any other gift that is offered to us as we go through life, each of us has the option whether to receive or to reject this unique gift that embodies the reality of an eternity with God.

John further explains that:

> "He who has the Son has life; he who does not have the Son of God does not have life. I write these things to you who believe in the name of the Son of God so that you may know that you have eternal life" (1 John 5:12-13).

God has a desire for every human being to hear and receive this life-transforming message of salvation, but we all have free wills and the ability to make our own choices.

Paul, writing in 1 Timothy 2:3-4, shares with us a piece of God's heart as indicated:

> "This is good, and pleases God our Savior, who wants all men to be saved and to come to a knowledge of the truth."

The message of salvation through the preaching of the gospel must, therefore, reach to the billions of human beings on this planet who are scattered over every continent, country, island or cay, living in the mountains, valleys and plains.

From Jesus' instructions in Acts 1:7-8, it is clear that though the preaching of the gospel would begin in Jerusalem, the ultimate plan of God was that it would reach to the ends of the earth.

We also know from 2 Peter 3:9 that:

> "The Lord is not slow in keeping his promise, as some understand slowness. He is patient with you, not wanting anyone to perish, but everyone to come to repentance."

According to Romans 3:10 and 23, the unpleasant truth is that:

> "There is no one righteous , not even one."

"For all have sinned and fall short of the glory of God."

It follows, then, that all people everywhere are in need of God's salvation, without which they will face eternal destruction.

This is why we are told in 2 Peter 3:9, that God is patient (longsuffering) and does not want anyone to be lost or to die in his/her sins, but desires that everyone should repent, accept his gift of eternal life and be eternally saved.

The Old Testament prophet, Ezekiel, clearly expresses God's compassionate heart as he appeals to his wayward people:

> "Say to them, As surely as I live, declares the Sovereign Lord, I take no pleasure in the death of the wicked, but rather that they turn from their ways and live. Turn! Turn from your evil ways! Why will you die, O house of Israel?" (Ezekiel 33:11).

From as far back as the time of Abraham, it was clear from the Scriptures (Genesis 12:3), that God's intention was to bless all the nations (ethnic groups, peoples) of the earth.

It was God who designed the world and established, according to Paul:

> "every nation of men, that they should inhabit the whole earth; and he determined the times set for them and the exact places where they should live" (Acts 17:26).

It is not surprising, then, that God wants his gospel message to reach to all people, everywhere, because it is only through this gospel that righteousness is imparted, so that people may be saved (Romans 1:16-17).

We who claim to be the witnesses (disciples, followers) of Jesus Christ (Acts 1:8) must be willing to carry this gospel to the very ends of the earth, even risking our lives like Paul (Acts 20:22-24, 21:12-14, 2 Corinthians 11:23-33) as we go into strange and unfamiliar territories.

The truth is that, if we are not willing to obey Jesus' Great Commission, then we have not yet understood God's merciful and compassionate heart for mankind.

If we have no concern, desire or passion for the evangelization of lost people, all across this globe, then, can we really claim to be authentic witnesses (disciples, followers) of Jesus Christ?

If the hurting, harassed, helpless, homeless, heartless, hopeless people of this world mean nothing more to us than mere statistics, and if their spiritual blindness does not disturb us, then our own salvation becomes suspect.

If our primary purpose on this earth is to enjoy life with our family and friends, and to acquire real estate and financial wealth, then could it be that some of us, without realizing it, have seriously lost our way?

It is imperative that we have the same attitude to those in need of salvation as God does, and that we are willing to participate in the process of world evangelization and missions, while we have the ability to do so.

There are countless opportunities to go, to give, to pray and to evangelize until the job gets done ... before the Lord returns.

Have you ever seriously considered what role God requires you to play, in the global transmission of this gospel?

What part are you presently playing?

What additional dimensions do you intend to explore as you contemplate the uncertain future, and our need to reach the lost at any cost?

CHAPTER 2

From Every Tribe, Language, People, Nation

"And they sang a new song: You are worthy to take the scroll and to open its seals, because you were slain, and with your blood you purchased men for God from every tribe and language and people and nation" (Rev.5:9).

When this present dispensation is over we, like John, will discover that those who have been redeemed (purchased by the blood of Jesus Christ), have come from every kind of socio-economic, ethnic, racial, cultural and geographical backgrounds.

There is no tribe, language, people or nation that has been exempted from the saving grace of Almighty God.

All people, everywhere, from every conceivable location on the globe will one day realize that:

"Salvation is found in no one else, for there is no other name under heaven given to men by which we must be saved" (Acts 4:12).

We also observe in Revelation chapter 7:9 that there was:

"a great multitude that no one could count, from every nation, tribe, people and language, standing before the throne and in front of the Lamb".

We do not know precisely how God will deal with all those in the "distant times" and "distant places" who have never heard the gospel message and who, therefore, died without a personal relationship with Jesus Christ.

These difficult matters we will leave to the compassionate, all-wise, omniscient, omnipotent Creator of the universe to address.

What we are, however, clear about is that the present Church (of which we are a part) still has an unfinished mandate to preach the gospel to every creature, so that people may be redeemed from, "Every tribe, language, people and nation" and be reconciled to their God… for all eternity.

This reminds us that Jesus' disciples were commissioned to be his witnesses, " in Jerusalem, and in all Judea and Samaria, and to the ends of the earth" (Acts 1:8).

This goal was to take priority over and above any unhealthy interest in times and dates, or in the establishment of any earthly, political kingdoms.

Jesus (according to Matthew 24:14) in a partial response to a series of questions pertaining to the "end times" (eschatology) and his "return" (parousia) told his disciples:

> "And this gospel of the kingdom will be preached in the whole world as a testimony to all nations, and then the end will come."

It may be observed that all these references point to either the uniqueness of Jesus Christ or the universality of the gospel message, and that all people (everyone) everywhere should have the opportunity to hear (and respond to) this gospel at least once in their lifetime.

It is also important to understand that the Greek word, "ethnos", which is often translated as "nations" or "whole world", literally means "ethnic groups", "people groups" or "peoples".

One of the most valuable questions to be answered, as we engage in World Evangelism and missions is: "What is the best spoken language to be used in reaching the "nations" of the world with the gospel message?"

Some zealous Christian ministers may favor the English language because of its international status, while others may select Spanish, being the most wide-spread, or French, German, Hindi, Swahili, Japanese, Mandarin or even Greek.

The truth is, however, that the best language with which to reach any group of un-evangelized or unsaved people is the particular language of that ethnic group. We must learn to speak the same language that they are already speaking, if we expect to communicate effectively with them.

It follows, then, that if we are serious about fulfilling Jesus' Great Commission, we must patiently consider the language and culture of those to whom the gospel is to be transmitted.

The word "culture" is of particular significance whenever the gospel is being proclaimed across political, geographical and national boundaries.

Not only should we strive to understand our own culture, but we also have a responsibility to appreciate and respect the cultural beliefs and practices of other ethnic groups as we purposefully interact with them.

The following definitions of "culture" should provide some helpful insights and perspectives for all who truly desire to see the whole world evangelized, in keeping with God's expressed will.

> "Culture is a very inclusive word. It takes into account linguistic, political, economic, social, psychological, religious, national, racial, and other differences." (David J. Hesselgrave, p. C35)

> "Culture is a way of thinking, feeling, believing. It is the group's knowledge stored up for future use." (Clyde Kluckhohn, p.C35)

PURPOSEFUL EVANGELISM AND MISSIONS

"Culture is a design for living. It is a plan according to which society adapts itself to its physical, social, and ideational environment." (Louis Luzbetak, p.C35)

The above definitions were drawn from the text: Perspectives on the World Christian Movement, Revised Edition, 1992, Edited by Ralph D. Winter and Steven C. Hawthorne, Published by William Carey Library, Pasadena, California, U.S.A.

For further discussions on this subject, with realistic and thought-provoking illustrations, please see both Chapter 10 and Appendix 1.

It may also prove helpful to formulate your own definition of "culture", based on your exposure through reading and personal experiences, bearing in mind such concepts as; norms, societal values, ethnic distinctives, spoken languages, customs, religious practices, sporting activities, artistic expressions, moral taboos and corporate identity.

These are certainly some of the vital areas for consideration, study and exploration as the authentic Christian witness seeks to successfully evangelize every tribe, language, people and nation with the gospel of Jesus Christ.

There are still millions of un-evangelized people throughout the world, particularly in Muslim-dominated territories, communist countries, and animistic societies, especially in the region defined by the "10/40 Window" (further research recommended) in addition to those within secular humanistic strongholds.

Since each human soul is important to Almighty God (Luke 9:25, 15:1-32), it therefore follows that every possible effort must be made to penetrate the various cultures with the gospel, even if I have to:

"become all things to all men, so that by all possible means I might save some" (1 Corinthians 9:22).

We must be prepared, as compassionate ministers of the

gospel, to make personal sacrifices that transcend our comfort zones and which may involve the retraining of our minds, deepening of spiritual convictions and willing expenditure of our financial resources.

CHAPTER 3

And This Gospel of The Kingdom

"And this gospel of the kingdom will be preached in the whole world as a testimony to all nations, and then the end will come" (Matthew 24:14).

The nations (Greek: *ethnos*) of this world are in desperate need of the life-transforming gospel of Jesus Christ, which provides the only means of salvation for the lost, and genuine, spiritual empowerment for the converted.

Paul declared unapologetically in Romans 1:16-17:

"I am not ashamed of the gospel, because it is the power of God for the salvation of everyone who believes: first for the Jew, then fopr the Gentile. For in the gospel, a righteousness from God is revealed, a righteousness that is by faith from first to last, just as it is written: The righteous will live by faith."

His commitment to this gospel is also expressed in 1 Corinthians 9:16-17:

"Yet when I preach the gospel, I cannot boast, for I am compelled to preach. Woe to me if I do not preach the gospel! If I preach voluntarily, I have a reward; if not voluntarily, I am simply discharging the trust committed to me."

The gospel message speaks to us about salvation, but it also presents to us the lordship of Jesus Christ and the spiritual kingdom over which he rules by the power of his Holy Spirit and through his blood-redeemed people.

The gospel is therefore sometimes referred to as the *gospel of the kingdom*, as already observed in Matthew 24:14

Mark 13:10 also tells us:

"And the gospel must first be preached to all nations."

It is easy to see, from these and several other passages, that God has a vested interest in all the nations (peoples) of the earth, and desires that all should hear the gospel message, before Jesus returns to judge, rule and reign.

Please observe that the essentials of the gospel are summarized by Paul in 1 Corinthians 15:1-4, as the death, burial and resurrection of Jesus Christ, according to the Scriptures.

He also warns us to be careful about those who are trying to preach another or a different gospel (2 Corinthians 11:1-4, Galatians 1:6-9).

Those who engage in such counter-productive activities are definitely not to be encouraged or embraced.

Paul's own evaluation of this deceptive practice in the Body of Christ led him to a decisive conclusion, as follows:

"I am astonished that you are so quickly deserting the one who called you by the grace of Christ and are turning to a different gospel – which is really no gospel at all.

Evidently some people are throwing you into confusion and are trying to pervert the gospel of Christ.

AND THIS GOSPEL OF THE KINGDOM

But even if we or an angel from heaven should preach a gospel other than the one we preached to you, let him be eternally condemned!

As we have already said, so now I say again: if anybody is preaching to you a gospel other than what you accepted, let him be eternally condemned!" (Gal. 1:6-9).

The gospel that we preach, if it is authentic, will lead people into a genuine, personal relationship with Jesus Christ.

This salvation will be received only on the basis of faith in the redemptive work of Jesus Christ, which was completed 2000 years ago, when on Calvary's cross he declared; "tetelestai!" (John 19:30) ...meaning "paid in full", or "completely complete" or "it is finished).

The Scriptures make it abundantly clear that it is only on the basis of this simple, child-like faith that Jesus' salvation can be activated:

"For it is by grace you have been saved, through faith – and this is not from yourselves, it is the gift of God – not by works, so that no one can boast" (Ephesians 2:8-9).

"He saved us, not because of righteous things we had done, but because of his mercy. He saved us through the washing of rebirth and renewal by the Holy Spirit, whom he poured out on us generously through Jesus Christ our Savior, so that having been justified by his grace, we might become heirs having the hope of eternal life" (Titus 3:5-7).

"He then brought them out and asked, Sirs, what must I do to be saved? They replied, Believe in the Lord Jesus and you will be saved – you and your house" (Acts 16:30-31)

"That if you confess with your mouth, Jesus is Lord, and believe in your heart that God raised him from the dead, you will be saved. For it is with your heart that you believe and are justified, and it is with your mouth that you confess and are saved" (Romans 10:9-10).

"Just as Moses lifted up the snake in the desert, so the Son of Man must be lifted up, that everyone who believes in him may have eternal life" (John 3:14-15).

"He came to that which was his own, but his own did not receive him. Yet to all who received him, to those who believed in his name, he gave the right to become children of God – children born not of natural descent, nor of human decision or a husband's will, but born of God" (John 1:11-13).

"I tell you the truth, whoever hears my word and believes him who sent me has eternal life and will not be condemned; he has crossed over from death to life" (John 5:24).

This gospel of the kingdom should also help people to surrender to the lordship of Jesus Christ in all areas of their lives, and positively affect their families, communities and nations.

It is designed to become a catalyst for both personal and community transformation, since faith must be validated by its works, and genuine conversion should lead to moral introspection, spiritual empowerment and social engagement.

All who claim to be true disciples or followers (witnesses, ambassadors) of Jesus Christ must, therefore, be prepared to share the gospel of the kingdom through their words and their lives, to all who are willing to hear and accept the truth.

The whole world is crying out for answers to the escalating problems of war, criminal activity, moral depravity, natural disasters, corrupt governments, religious confusion and social disintegration.

We are assured, in the writings of Paul, that:

AND THIS GOSPEL OF THE KINGDOM

"the creation itself will be liberated from its bondage to decay and brought into the glorious freedom of the children of God. We know that the whole creation has been groaning as in the pains of childbirth right up to the present time" (Romans 8:21-22).

Peter encourages us, that:

"in keeping with his promise we are looking forward to a new heaven and a new earth, the home of righteousness" (2 Peter 3:13).

The prophet Isaiah, thousands of years ago, spoke of a glorious, peaceful day to come when:

"The wolf will live with the lamb, the leopard will lie down with the goat, the calf and the lion and the yearling together; and a little child will lead them.

The cow will feed with the bear, their young will lie down together, and the lion will eat straw like the ox.

The infant will play near the hole of the cobra, and the young child put his hands in the viper's nest.

They will neither harm nor destroy on all my holy mountain, for the earth will be full of the knowledge of the Lord as the waters cover the sea" (Isaiah 11:6-9).

John, while on the Isle of Patmos, also got a glimpse of the world to come:

"Then I saw a new heaven and a new earth, for the first heaven and the first earth had passed away, and there was no longer any sea.

I saw the Holy City, the new Jerusalem, coming down out of heaven from God, prepared as a bride beautifully dressed for her husband.

> And I heard a loud voice from the throne saying, Now the dwelling of God is with men, and he will live with them.
>
> They will be his people, and God himself will be with them and be their God. He will wipe every tear from their eyes.
>
> There will be no more death or mourning or crying or pain, for the old order of things has passed away" (Revelation 21:1-4).

Jesus, however, provided his disciples with a reality check in Matthew 24, explaining that before this present world culminates, there will be an extended season of spiritual deception, destructive wars, devastating natural disasters, increased wickedness and great, unequaled distress.

It is in the midst of painting this dreadful picture of a chaotic, intoxicated, deteriorating world, that he reminded his followers that:

> "This gospel of the kingdom will be preached in the whole world as a testimony to all nations, and then the end will come" (Matthew 24:14).

Those who claim allegiance with King Jesus and are recipients of his unmerited grace presently have the glorious opportunity of being a part of his unfolding script, in evangelizing this current generation.

It is definitely our responsibility to ensure that this gospel message reaches to the ends of the earth and permeates every ethnic group throughout the world, as the kingdom of God is being established and expanded.

CHAPTER 4

Through Jesus Christ Alone

"For God did not send his Son into the world to condemn the world, but to save the world through him" (John 3:17).

We have already argued that possibly the most well-known verse in the entire Bible is John 3:16, which tells us:

"For God so loved the world that he gave his one and only Son that whoever believes in him shall not perish but have eternal life."

As we continue to read verses 17 and 18, it becomes abundantly clear that God's Son did not come to condemn the world, but to save the world, and those who do not believe in him are already condemned because they have rejected the true Light.

We observe from several places, that Jesus understood quite well that he had a rescue mission to complete:

"Jesus said to him, Today salvation has come to this house, because this man, too, is a son of Abraham. For the Son of Man came to seek and to save what was lost" (Luke 19:9-10).

◄ **PURPOSEFUL EVANGELISM AND MISSIONS**

"And whoever wants to be the first among you must be your slave—just as the Son of Man did not come to be served, but to serve, and to give his life as a ransom for many" (Matthew 20:27-28).

"From that time on Jesus began to explain to his disciples that he must go to Jerusalem and suffer many things at the hands of the elders, chief priests and teachers of the law, and that he must be killed and on the third day be raised to life" (Matthew 16:21).

"For even the Son of Man did not come to be served, but to serve, and to give his life as a ransom for many" (Mark 10:45)

"Jesus replied, The hour has come for the Son of Man to be glorified.

I tell you the truth, unless a kernel of wheat falls to the ground and dies, it remains only a single seed. But if it dies, it produces many seeds.

The man who loves his life will lose it, while the man who hates his life in this world will keep it for eternal life...

Now my heart is troubled, and what shall I say? Father, save me from this hour? No, it was for this very reason I came to this hour" (John 12:23-27).

"Then he opened their minds so they could understand the Scriptures. He told them, This is what is written. The Christ will suffer and rise from the dead on the third day, and repentance and forgiveness of sins will be preached in his name to all nations, beginning at Jerusalem" (Luke 24:45-47).

One of our major tasks as obedient Christians is to effectively

THROUGH JESUS CHRIST ALONE

present the undiluted gospel message to the entire world, declaring that Jesus Christ is the true "Light" and the only credible means of experiencing eternal life.

We have not been called to become a part of the Ecumenical Movement but have, instead, been given a mandate to engage in deliberate, purposeful World Evangelization.

Please be reminded that Ecumenism teaches (among other things) that Jesus Christ is just one of the countless avatars of light (or messiahs), that all people everywhere will ultimately be saved by trusting in their own "lights", and that Christians should embrace and endorse all other religions, instead of evangelizing the nations (as Jesus commanded).

The Bible repeatedly affirms that salvation (eternal life) comes through faith in Jesus Christ, alone.

Consider the following examples:

a) John 14:6

"Jesus answered, I am the way and the truth and the life. No one comes to the Father except through me."

b) Acts 4:12

"Salvation is found in no one else, for there is no other name under heaven given to men by which we must be saved."

c) 1 Timothy 2:3-6

"Now that you have tasted that the Lord is good. As you come to him, the living Stone – rejected by men but chosen by God and precious to him – you also, like living stones, are being built into a spiritual house to be a holy priesthood, offering spiritual sacrifices acceptable to God through Jesus Christ.

For in Scripture it says: See, I lay in Zion, a chosen and

precious cornerstone, and the one who trusts in him will never be put to shame."

d) 1 Peter 1:18-20

"For you know that it was not with perishable things such as silver or gold that you were redeemed from the empty way of life handed down to you from your forefathers, but with the precious blood of Christ, a lamb without blemish or defect. He was chosen before the creation of the world, but was revealed in these last times for your sake."

e) 1 John 2:1-2

"My dear children, I write this to you so that you will not sin. But if anybody does sin, we have one who speaks to the Father in our defense – Jesus Christ, the Righteous One. He is the atoning sacrifice (propitiation) for our sins, and not only for ours but also for the sins of the whole world."

f) Galatians 4:4-5

"But when the time had fully come, God sent his Son, born of a woman, born under law, to redeem those under law, that we might receive the full rights of sons."

If salvation could be found by sincerely believing in whomever or whatever we desire, then there would be no need for Jesus Christ to die on that cruel cross, 2000 years ago.

John the Baptist made no mistake when he identified Jesus, on at least two occasions, as the Lamb of God:

"The next day John saw Jesus coming toward him and said, Look, the Lamb of God, who takes away the sin of the world" (John 1:29).

"The next day John was there again with two of his disciples. When he saw Jesus passing by, he said, Look, the Lamb of God" (John 1:35-36).

The angel of the Lord was not telling lies when he instructed Joseph:

"Joseph son of David, do not be afraid to take Mary home as your wife, because what is conceived in her is from the Holy Spirit. She will give birth to a son, and you are to give him the name Jesus, because he will save his people from their sins" (Matthew 1:21).

Paul was not confused, when in speaking of Jesus Christ, he said:

"Consequently, just as the result of one trespass was condemnation for all men, so also the result of one act of righteousness was justification that brings life for all men. For just as through the disobedience of the one man the many were made sinners, so also through the obedience of the one man many will be made righteous" (Romans 5:18-19).

The writer to the Hebrews was certainly not double minded when he wrote about Christ saying:

"Day after day every priest stands and performs his religious duties; again and again he offers the same sacrifices, which can never take away sins. But when this priest had offered for all time one sacrifice for sins, he sat down at the right hand of God. Since that time he waits for his enemies to be made his footstool, because by one sacrifice he has made perfect forever those who are being made holy" (Hebrews 10:11-14).

John, based on his revelation from God on the Isle of Patmos, knew that there was only one person who could fit the following description:

PURPOSEFUL EVANGELISM AND MISSIONS

"Then one of the elders said to me, Do not weep! See, the Lion of the tribe of Judah, the Root of David, has triumphed. He is able to open the scroll and its seven seals.

Then I saw a Lamb, looking as if it had been slain, standing in the center of the throne, encircled by the four living creatures and the elders...

And when he had taken it, the four living creatures and the twenty-four elders fell down before the Lamb...

And they sang a new song: You are worthy to take the scroll and to open its seals, because you were slain, and with your blood you purchased men for God from every tribe and language and people and nation.

You have made them to be a kingdom and priests to serve our God, and they will reign on the earth" (Revelation 5:5-10).

If Buddha, Krishna, Mohammed, Haile Selassie, Sai Baba, Confucius, Zoroaster, L. Ron Hubbard, Joseph Smith, Mary Baker Eddy, St. Germaine, or even the Virgin Mary could qualify as Savior, then Jesus could easily have been prevented from going through an ordeal in which:

"His appearance was so disfigured beyond that of any man and his form marred beyond human likeness" (Isaiah 52:14).

"He had no beauty or majesty to attract us to him, nothing in his appearance that we should desire him. He was despised and rejected by men, a man of sorrows, and familiar with suffering.

Like one from whom men hide their faces he was despised, and we esteemed him not. Surely he took up our sins and carried our sorrows, yet we considered him stricken by God, smitten by him, and afflicted.

But he was pierced for our transgressions, he was crushed for our iniquities; the punishment that brought us peace was upon him, and by his wounds we are healed.

We all, like sheep, have gone astray, each of us has turned to his own way; and the Lord has laid on him the iniquity of us all" (Isaiah 53:2-6).

There is no other human being who has lived on this planet who can genuinely claim the following credentials:

"Therefore let all Israel be assured of this: God has made this Jesus, whom you crucified, both Lord and Christ" (Acts 2:36).

"God made him who had no sin to be sin for us, so that in him we might become the righteousness of God" (2 Corinthians 5:21).

"When Christ came as high priest of the good things that are already here, he went through the greater and more perfect tabernacle that is not man-made, that is to say, not a part of this creation. He did not enter by means of the blood of goats and calves; but he entered the Most Holy Place once for all by his own blood, having obtained eternal redemption" (Hebrews 9: 11-12).

"Your attitude should be the same as that of Jesus Christ; Who, being in very nature God, did not consider equality with God something to be grasped, but made himself nothing, taking the very nature of a servant, being made in human likeness,

And being found in appearance as a man, he humbled himself and became obedient to death – even death on a cross!

> Therefore God exalted him to the highest place and gave him the name that is above every name, that at the name of Jesus every knee should bow, in heaven and on earth and under the earth, and every tongue confess that Jesus Christ is Lord, to the glory of God the Father" (Philippians 2:5-11).

It is through the good news of this Jesus who died, was buried and rose again for our salvation, that the people of this world can be reconciled to their heavenly Father.

If salvation could be obtained without genuine acceptance of this gospel message, and if "Anonymous Christians" really existed, then there would definitely be no need to evangelize the nations of the world.

Since, however, the gospel is still the only power of God unto salvation, to all who believe (Rom. 1:16), then those who are authentic Christians have no other option but to preach the death, burial and resurrection of Jesus Christ (1 Corinthians 15:3-4) to the spiritually lost, wherever they are located.

We are responsible to ensure that repentance and forgiveness of sins are preached in his name (Luke 24:47), wherever we go, to all creation (Mark 16:15) and in all nations (Matthew 28:19).

We can easily get distracted (like the Jews) looking for miraculous signs or like the Greeks (seeking after human wisdom) ... or we can decide, like Paul, to preach Christ crucified (1 Corinthians 1:22-23).

Which option will you choose to take? Which Lord will you seek to glorify? Which kingdom will you strive to build?

CHAPTER 5

But The Workers Are Few

> "Then he said to his disciples, The harvest is plentiful but the workers are few" (Matthew 9:37).

There are over six billion people in the world today, the majority of which have not yet surrendered their lives to Jesus Christ; including several millions who have never heard the gospel message or even seen a copy of the Bible, written in their own language or dialect.

An enormous amount of work still needs to be done, if we intend to faithfully obey Jesus' commission to "make disciples of all nations".

The report in Matthew 9:35-36 shows clearly that Jesus was filled with compassion for the crowds of harassed, helpless people of his day, because they were "like sheep without a shepherd".

This heartfelt concern for the lost, suffering, disoriented multitudes led him to instruct his disciples:

> "...The harvest is plentiful but the workers are few. Ask the Lord of the harvest, therefore, to send out workers into his harvest field" (Matthew 9:37-38).

As we consider the vast harvest field that exists in the 21st Century, the challenge is even greater to find appropriate, competent, willing workers for the job.

Where, then, are these workers to be found, and in what ways are we being called to be part of this life-saving labor force?

Could it be that there is a specific call on our own life, and that God wants to use you as a trail-blazer, pioneer, prototype or even a martyr for the kingdom's sake?

It might be that you are one of those disciples who were called into a (behind-the-scenes) ministry of intense and continuous intercession for the workers who are laboring in the harvest field.

Did you notice, however, that as the episode unfolded into Matthew Chapter 10, the same disciples who were told to intercede for workers, were later empowered by Jesus, and carefully commissioned to go "to the lost sheep of Israel", preaching the message: "The kingdom of heaven is near"?

It seems, from all indications, that even those who pray privately will also need to share the gospel publicly, and many who consider themselves to be "specialist intercessors" should also remain in readiness, if called upon, to proclaim God's word with the same intense passion with which they pray.

Even though each believer has been given specific and differing spiritual gifts (1 Corinthians 12:1-31, Romans 12:3-8, Ephesians 4: 7-16, 1 Peter 4:10-11), we are still expected to do the work of an evangelist, finding witnessing opportunities... in every conceivable situation.

The truth is that; intercession and evangelism are not mutually exclusive, but complimentary activities. The one who is called to "stand in the gap" is also often called to "preach the gospel" and to "set the captives free".

What we, however, find in response to God's call for action, is often a barrage of well articulated, even legitimate-sounding, excuses.

What are some of the most common excuses that the people around you give in response to God's call on their lives?

As we observe our fellow human beings in the biblical records, we notice that they too, often had their "plausible" excuses. Moses, for example, reasoned with God:

"Who am I, that I should go to Pharaoh and bring the Israelites out of Egypt?" (Exodus 3:11)

"Suppose I go to the Israelites and say to them, The God of your fathers has sent me to you, and they ask me, What is his name? Then what shall I tell them?" (Exodus 3:13)

"What if they do not believe me or listen to me and say, The Lord did not appear to you?" (Exodus 4:1)

"O Lord, I have never been eloquent neither in the past nor since you have spoken to your servant. I am slow of speech and tongue" (Exodus 4:10).

"O Lord, please send someone else to do it" (Exodus 4:13).

Moses had good, logical reasons not to go on this mission, especially since he would have to face the Israelites and to confront Pharaoh on his own turf in Egypt, after the unresolved murder some 40 years before.

Even though Moses was now a stuttering, desert-dwelling fugitive, God was still insistent:

"The cry of the Israelites has reached me, and I have seen the way the Egyptians are oppressing them. So now go, I am sending you to Pharaoh to bring my people the Israelites out of Egypt" (Exodus 3:9-10).

The report tells us that, as a result of the many excuses of inadequacy, insecurity, fear, lack of eloquence and slowness of speech:

"The Lord's anger burned against Moses" (Exodus 4:14).

PURPOSEFUL EVANGELISM AND MISSIONS

It finally dawned on Moses that he was speaking to the Sovereign God who controls life, speech, sight and circumstances, and who had already made the un-reversible declaration:

> "I have indeed seen the misery of my people in Egypt. I have heard them crying out because of their slave drivers, and I am concerned about their suffering. So I have come down to rescue them from the hand of the Egyptians and to bring them up out of that land into a good and spacious land, a land flowing with milk and honey..." (Exodus 3:7-8).

Regardless of Moses' numerous excuses, he eventually realized that he had an unchanging, non-negotiable commission to go, and as is often said... "the rest is history".

In Judges 6, we encounter another nervous, fearful candidate who, "was threshing wheat in a winepress to keep it from the Midianites" (Judges 6:11).

The angel of the Lord confidently greeted Gideon, declaring:

> "The Lord is with you, mighty warrior...Go in the strength you have and save Israel out of Midian's hand. Am I not sending you?" (Judges 6:12-14)

You will, however, observe Gideon's *reasonable* excuses:

> "But sir...if the Lord is with us, why has all this happened to us? Where are all the wonders that our fathers told us about when they said, Did not the Lord bring us up out of Egypt? But now the Lord has abandoned us and put us into the hand of Midian" (Judges 6:13).

> "But Lord...How can I save Israel? My clan is the weakest in Manasseh, and I am the least in my family (Judges 6:15).

In spite of these realities, God had a definite call on Gideon's life and assured him:

"I will be with you, and you will strike down all the Midianites together" (Judges 6:16).

As a result of Gideon's subsequent obedience to his call, we are told ...not only of his miraculous, comprehensive victory over the Midianites (Judges 7), but also of his inclusion in the "Hall of Faith" (Hebrews 11:32).

Jeremiah, the prophet, also had a significant call to action from God, but his honest response was:

"Ah, Sovereign Lord...I do not know how to speak: I am only a child" (Jeremiah 1:6).

God was, however, neither touched, impressed nor silenced by this excuse of inadequacy, inexperience, youthfulness or his inability to speak.

Jeremiah, like all of us, needed to be reminded that whenever there is an important assignment to be executed, then God will always make it possible for us to do our part.

The Lord, therefore, rebuked, encouraged and commissioned him:

"Do not say, I am only a child. You must go to everyone I send you to and say whatever I command you. Do not be afraid of them, for I am with you and will rescue you" (Jeremiah 1:7-8).

"Now I have put my words in your mouth. See, today I appoint you over nations and kingdoms to uproot and tear down, to destroy and overthrow, to build and to plant" (Jeremiah 1:9-10)

Isaiah's call to ministry also came in the midst of controversial circumstances, where the prophet himself recognized his "unworthiness" to serve as God's mouthpiece. His desperate reaction to God's vision was:

"Woe to me! ... I am ruined! For I am a man of unclean lips, and I live among a people of unclean lips, and my eyes have seen the King, the Lord Almighty" (Isaiah 6:5).

In spite of this true confession, God neither backed off nor changed his mind about his choice. He simply addressed the issue in question, so that the mission could proceed:

"Then one of the seraphs flew to me with a live coal in his hand, which he had taken with tongs from the altar. With it he touched my mouth and said, See, this has touched your lips; and your guilt is taken away and your sin atoned for" (Isaiah 6:6-7).

When the voice of the Lord later called, "Whom shall I send? And whom will go for us?" ... the quick response that came from the confident, consecrated servant was:

"Here am I. Send me!" (Isaiah 6:8)

The run-away prophet, Jonah, also had his share of excuses when called by God to:

"Go to the great city of Nineveh and preach against it, because its wickedness has come up before me" (Jonah 1:2).

Jonah made no attempt to argue with God as Moses did, nor to plead inadequacy or inability as Gideon, Jeremiah or Isaiah had done. He simply turned in the opposite direction and fled with all his might towards Tarshish.

As the story unfolds, however, we discover that his erratic behavior had been fueled by a deep- rooted mindset, expressed in his own words:

"O Lord, is this not what I said when I was still at home? This is why I was so quick to flee to Tarshish. I knew that you are a gracious and compassionate God, slow to anger and abounding in love, a God who relents from sending calamity. Now, O Lord, take away my life, for it is better for me to die than to live. (Jonah 4:2-3).

Jonah's excuse for both his initial disobedience and subsequent displeasure and anger, was that he wanted the wicked to receive God's harsh judgment, instead of his gracious forgiveness.

He would rather to see the "more than a hundred and twenty thousand people who cannot tell their right hand from their left" (Jonah 4:11) perish under God's wrath than to be pardoned and transformed by God's love.

Is this the kind of heart that we should have towards humanity, considering that:

"There is no one righteous, not even one" (Romans 3:10).

"All have sinned and fall short of the glory of God" (Romans 3:23).

"If any one of you is without sin, let him be the first to throw a stone at her" (John 8:7).

"If we claim to be without sin, we deceive ourselves and the truth is not in us… If we claim we have not sinned, we make him out to be a liar and his word has no place in our lives" (1 John 1:8-10).

We who have been redeemed by the blood of Jesus Christ, regenerated by God's Holy Spirit and restored to God by the message of his grace, must be careful that we do not become like the "unmerciful servant":

"Then the master called the servant in. You wicked servant, he said, I cancelled all that debt of yours because you begged me to. Shouldn't you have had mercy on your fellow servant just as I had on you? In anger his master turned him over to the jailers to be tortured, until he should pay back all he owed" (Matthew 18:32-34).

Let us never forget that there were multitudes of God's people who took the time to intercede for us and made undisclosed sacrifices on our behalf, so that we were able to hear and receive the life-transforming gospel of Jesus Christ.

We who have been shown mercy, and reconciled by God's grace, have now been given the "ministry" and "message of reconciliation" as "Christ's ambassadors" (1 Timothy 1:12-16, 2 Corinthians 5:17-20).

It is a dangerous thing to shrink back and make unwarranted excuses, especially in the light of the following quote, attributed to Dr. D. James Kennedy (Founder of Evangelism Explosion International III).

"An excuse is the skin of a reason…stuffed with a lie".

There were several potential disciples whom Jesus called, according to Luke 9:59-61, but they too, had their excuses.

"Lord, first let me go and bury my father."

"I will follow you, Lord; but first let me go back and say good-by to my family."

Those who were invited to the great banquet (Luke 14:15-24) also had their excuses:

"I have just bought a field, and I must go and see it. Please excuse me."

"I have just bought five yoke of oxen, and I'm on my way to try them out. Please excuse me."

"I just got married, so I can't come."

As we consider Jesus' Great Commission and the urgent need for workers, how will you respond? Do you have an excuse? What is it? How well can it stand against the truth of God's Word?

When, for example, was the last time that you started a conversation with a non-Christian and purposefully shared the Gospel with him/her? How recently have you led someone in a prayer of commitment or recommitment to the Lord Jesus Christ?

What really is your response to the vast harvest field of harassed, helpless people who are on a slippery, spiraling road, heading full speed towards a Christ-less, eternal hell fire?

CHAPTER **6**

Empowered To Be Witnesses

"He said to them: It is not for you to know the times or dates the Father has set by his own authority. But you will receive power when the Holy Spirit comes on you; and you will be my witnesses in Jerusalem, and in all Judea and Samaria, and to the ends of the earth" (Acts 1: 7-8).

Jesus' parting words to his faithful disciples, according to Acts 1:7-8, indicated that their ability to be effective witnesses would significantly depend on the Holy Spirit's empowerment and guidance.

We also observe the following, in Luke 24:47-49:

> "And repentance and forgiveness of sins will be preached in his name to all nations, beginning at Jerusalem. You are witnesses of these things. I am going to send you what my Father has promised; but stay in the city until you have been clothed with power from on high."

Jesus expected them (and us) to be effective communicators or transmitters of the gospel message, but he never gave a list of the methods or strategies that were to be used.

Why do you believe they were mandated to share the gospel as witnesses to all the nations of the world, yet without being given

PURPOSEFUL EVANGELISM AND MISSIONS

a missions handbook, a how-to-do-it manual or any systematic training in standard evangelistic procedures?

Christian leaders and churches over the centuries, have developed numerous programs, methods, strategies and ministries, including: personal evangelism, mass evangelism, crusade evangelism, friendship evangelism, presence evangelism, power evangelism, literature evangelism, tele-evangelism, cyber- evangelism, child evangelism, sports evangelism, concert evangelism, prison evangelism, hospital evangelism, student evangelism, camp evangelism… and the list continues.

While evangelistic methods keep changing, the evangelistic mandate and message remain the same as found in the New Testament, and must be directed by God's Holy Spirit.

We will discover, as we study the book of Acts, that the early disciples did not have committee meetings to plan evangelistic strategies, but they shared the gospel wherever they went, as led by the Holy Spirit.

What we witness, there, is not the intellectual genius of a few highly trained, theologically educated believers, but rather, the demonstration of God's presence and power at work, in spite of human limitations and weaknesses … to carry out his eternal purposes.

The Acts 1:8 imperative set the tone for the book of Acts and provided the impetus for a bunch of unlearned and despised Jewish disciples to eventually turn the world "upside down".

God definitely wanted these waiting disciples, who were to carry his precious gospel to the ends of the earth, to clearly understand that this mission was not one that depended on human knowledge, wisdom, ability or strategy, but on the Spirit's power.

Their subsequent infilling and empowerment by the Holy Spirit provided an experiential understanding of Jesus' words in Acts 1:8, and gradually convinced them that it didn't matter too much who, what or where they were, but rather … whose they were.

They had been sent on a mission for God, and it was that

same God who would accompany them, live in them, empower them and work through them, since he has a vested interest in the redemption of a world which he, himself, created.

The marvelous, miraculous, mind-boggling upper room "explosion" of Acts 2 should, therefore, not be seen as simply an ecstatic, emotional experience to cheer up some disheartened disciples, or to provide an entertaining sideshow for the thousands of Jewish visitors who had come to celebrate Pentecost.

God was, obviously, doing much more and he had a significantly greater goal in mind. There was a lost world, sinking in sin, that could only be reached by consecrated, committed Christians who were empowered by the Holy Spirit.

The early disciples, themselves, understood that the empowerment (or infilling or baptism) of the Holy Spirit was essential for successful evangelism and missions, especially in the context of our human limitations and the reality of ongoing demonic resistance and satanic power confrontations.

In Acts 2:42-47, the disciples lived as they were empowered and led by the Holy Spirit. Some of the visible results were:

"Everyone was filled with awe, and many wonders and miraculous signs were done by the apostles" (Acts 2:43).

"...The Lord added to their number daily those who were being saved" (Acts 2:47).

We also note that in Acts 8:14-19 (in Samaria), Acts 10:44-48 (at Cornelius' home) and Acts 19:1-6 (in Ephesus), different groups of "new converts" had special supernatural experiences, similar to that of Acts 2, in which they also "received the Holy Spirit" before being released as witnesses of Jesus Christ.

In two of these cases (Acts 8 and 19), hands had actually been laid on them by the visiting apostle(s), immediately after their conversion, producing visible, instantaneous results.

This was also a significant part of the responsibility given by

◄ **PURPOSEFUL EVANGELISM AND MISSIONS**

God to Ananias in Acts 9:10-17, concerning Saul of Tarsus (who later became Paul, the apostle) in the light of his being called as "a chosen vessel" to carry Jesus' name "before the Gentiles and their kings and before the people of Israel".

We are reminded of Paul's instructive words in 1 Corinthians 2:1-5:

> "When I came to you, brothers, I did not come with eloquence or superior wisdom as I proclaimed to you the testimony about God.
>
> For I resolved to know nothing while I was with you except Jesus Christ and him crucified.
>
> I came to you in weakness and fear, and with much trembling.
>
> My message and my preaching were not with wise and persuasive words, but with a demonstration of the Spirit's power, so that your faith might not rest on men's wisdom, but on God's power."

We recall the episode in Acts 4: 23-31, where the believers in the early church gathered together for prayer after Peter and John were released by the chief priests and Jewish elders.

Their passionate prayers ended on the following note:

> "Now, Lord, consider their threats and enable your servants to speak your word with great boldness. Stretch out your hand to heal and perform miraculous signs and wonders through the name of your holy servant Jesus" (Acts 4:29-30).

There was an immediate response from God:

> "After they prayed, the place where they were meeting was shaken. And they were all filled with the Holy Spirit and

spoke the word of God boldly" (Acts 4:31).

This experience resulted in a series of outcomes, including :

"With great power the apostles continued to testify to the resurrection of the Lord Jesus, and much grace was upon them all" (Acts 4:33).

By the time the story unfolds in Acts 5, we discover:

"The apostles performed many miraculous signs and wonders among the people" (Acts 5:12).

"Nevertheless, more and more men and women believed in the Lord and were added to their number" (Acts 5:14).

"As a result people brought the sick into the streets and laid them on beds and mats so that at least Peter's shadow might fall on some of them as he passed by" (Acts 5:15).

"Crowds gathered also from the towns around Jerusalem, bringing their sick and those tormented by evil spirits, and all of them were healed" (Acts 5:16).

The writer, in Acts 8:6, further observed:

"When the crowds heard Philip and saw the miraculous signs he did, they all paid close attention to what he said."

One does not have to be a rocket scientist, Rhode Scholar or New Testament Theologian to realize that the early disciples relied on the power and guidance of the Holy Spirit, instead of on their limited human intellect, abilities, wisdom or strategies.

As Paul and his team traveled on their various missionary journeys, they proved, beyond any shadow of a doubt that their dependence was completely on the indwelling Holy Spirit, by whom they had also been empowered.

◄ **PURPOSEFUL EVANGELISM AND MISSIONS**

In Acts 16, for example, it was the Holy Spirit who kept them "from preaching the word in the province of Asia" (Acts 16:6) and "would not allow them to" enter Bithynia (Acts 16:7).

It was, however, the same Sovereign Holy Spirit who subsequently spoke to Paul through a vision, indicating that it was now time to travel with the gospel into Macedonia (Acts 16: 9-10).

Successful evangelism and missions will not be accomplished until we allow God's Holy Spirit to empower and guide us in all of our initiatives.

If Paul had not known this truth before, he certainly would have discovered it during his brief encounter with Elymas (Bar-Jesus) the sorcerer, in Paphos.

The report tells us in Acts 13:6-12:

> "They travel through the whole island until they came to Paphos. There they met a Jewish sorcerer and false prophet named Bar-Jesus, who was an attendant of the proconsul, Sergius Paulus.
>
> The proconsul, an intelligent man, sent for Barnabas and Saul because he wanted to hear the word of God.
>
> But Elymas the sorcerer (for that is what his name means) opposed them and tried to turn the proconsul from the faith.
>
> Then Saul, who was also called Paul, filled with the Holy Spirit, looked straight at Elymas and said, You are a child of the devil and an enemy of everything that is right!
>
> You are full of all kinds of deceit and trickery. Will you never stop perverting the right ways of the Lord? Now the hand of the Lord is against you. You are going to be blind, and for a time you will be unable to see the light of the sun."
>
> Immediately mist and darkness came over him, and he

groped around, seeking someone to lead him by the hand.

When the proconsul saw what had happened, he believed, for he was amazed at the teaching about the Lord."

A frightened jailer and his entire household were also converted to the Christian faith because of a series of supernatural events in the city of Philippi; which started with the casting out of a demonic spirit from a slave girl, and culminated in an unnatural earthquake at midnight, in a prison cell.

Acts 16:30-34 provide for us the climax of this exciting encounter:

"He then brought them out and asked, Sirs, what must I do to be saved?

They replied, Believe in the Lord Jesus and you will be saved – you and your household.

Then they spoke the word of the Lord to him and to all the others in his house.

At that hour of the night the jailer took them and washed their wounds; then immediately he and all his family were baptized.

The jailer brought them into his house and set a meal before them; he was filled with joy because he had come to believe in God – he and his whole family."

As we reflect on the preceding passages, it becomes crystal clear that people will commit themselves to the Lord Jesus Christ, not because of our cute evangelistic strategies, but because of the supernatural work and convicting power of God's Holy Spirit.

CHAPTER 7

And These Signs Shall Accompany

> "Then the disciples went out and preached everywhere, and the Lord worked with them and confirmed his word by the signs that accompanied it" (Mark 16: 20).

Evangelism, as we should already know, is not supposed to be a boring, mechanical, religious duty, but an exciting, Spirit-led, daily adventure.

Wherever the Holy Spirit is at work through Jesus' disciples, proclaiming the gospel or rescuing the lost, we can expect to experience (or observe) a variety of supernatural, miraculous or unusual events, which serve to confirm the authenticity of God's Word.

Jesus had instructed his disciples, according to Mark 16: 15, to:

> "Go into all the world and preach the good news to all creation."

He further promised that:

> "These signs will accompany those who believe: In my name they will drive out demons; they will speak in new tongues; they will pick up snakes with their hands; and

when they drink deadly poison, it will not hurt them at all; they will place their hands on sick people, and they will get well" (Mark 16:17-18).

As you observe verse 20 you will find that the disciples went out in obedience to Jesus' instructions, and as they preached his word, then he confirmed it "by the signs that accompanied it".

This comes into sharper focus when we continue to explore the adventures of the early church as recorded in the book of Acts.

In Acts 14:3, for example, we find an almost identical statement:

"So Paul and Barnabas spent considerable time there, speaking boldly for the Lord, who confirmed the message of his grace by enabling them to do miraculous signs and wonders."

The account goes on to explain that in the city of Lystra, as "they continued to preach the good news" they encountered a man who had been "crippled in his feet, who was lame from birth and had never walked" (Acts 14:8).

In a relatively short period of time (recorded in verses 8 to 10) a miraculous healing took place. While listening to God's word, the man who had been crippled "had faith to be healed" and jumped up walking... in response to the disciples' command: "Stand up on your feet!"

One did not have to ask whether or not Paul and Barnabas got the people's attention, after such an amazing encounter.

The multitudes, we are told, were so shocked that they began shouting in their Lycaonian language that: "The gods have come down to us in human form!"

The miracle was so convincing that they even identified Barnabas and Paul as the gods, Zeus and Hermes, and started the process to offer worship to them.

This provided a golden opportunity for them to continue

preaching the gospel, to a receptive, captive audience, and so they declared with passion:

> "We are bringing you the good news, telling you to turn from these worthless things to the living God, who made heaven and earth and sea and everything in them.
>
> In the past he let nations go their own way. Yet he has not left himself without testimony: He has shown kindness by giving you rain from heaven and crops in their seasons; he provides you with plenty of food and fills your hearts with joy" (Acts 14:15-17).

If it had not been that some jealous Jews from Antioch and Iconium arrived there and confused the vulnerable, volatile crowds ... there is no telling how that episode could have ended, in terms of evangelistic success.

We recall that some time before, as Peter and John had been going up to the temple to pray, freshly baptized by the Holy Spirit, they too had encountered a man who was over forty years old, and who had also been crippled from birth.

As he looked at them, "expecting to get something from them", they instructed him: "In the name of Jesus Christ of Nazareth, walk" (Acts 3:5-6).

The report tells us that not only was the man miraculously healed, "walking and jumping and praising God" (Acts 3:8), and that the people "were filled with wonder and amazement at what had happened to him"(Acts 3:10), but that this provided an excellent preaching platform for Peter (Acts 3:11-26).

One of the direct outcomes from this series of events is that:

> "Many who heard the message believed, and the number of men grew to abut five thousand" (Acts 4: 4).

When God is allowed to show his miraculous power, such as supernaturally opening prison doors and releasing his faithful witnesses (Acts 5:17-26, Acts 12:1-19, Acts 16: 22–34), then even the skeptics and cynics will pay closer attention to those who speak God's word.

Let us be careful that we do not forget the instructive words found in Acts 8:6-8.

> "When the crowds heard Philip and saw the miraculous signs he did, they all paid close attention to what he said.
>
> With shrieks, evil spirits came out of many, and many paralytics and cripples were healed.
>
> So there was great joy in that city."

In Acts 9:32-33, we are told that while Peter was in Lydda, he found a man named Aeneas who was a paralytic and who was bedridden for eight years.

Immediately after the man had been instantly healed, according to verse 35:

> "All those who lived in Lydda and Sharon saw him and turned to the Lord."

We also know from Acts 9:36 – 41, about the miracle in Joppa, when a woman named Tabitha (or Dorcas) was raised from the dead.

According to verse 42, the immediate response of many people in that region was that they "believed in the Lord".

Paul declared that he "fought wild beasts in Ephesus" (1 Corinthians 15:32), living for three years in a city that was given over to the worship of the goddess Diana (Artemes), plagued with Jewish exorcists and practicing sorcerers.

He certainly needed to have God's supernatural endorsement on his ministry. Signs and wonders were, for him, not optional accessory, but vital parts of his artillery, as he sought to carry the gospel to the ends of the earth.

This was not the context in which one could simply share the "Four Spiritual Laws" or mechanically do the "Evangelism Explosion" presentation, and hope to hear an applause or to reap a bountiful harvest of souls.

Diabolic spiritual strongholds would first need to be demolished, principalities and powers disarmed and ground level demonic spirits confronted, before the disciples could even find a listening ear or a receptive heart.

One can understand, then, why:

> "God did extraordinary miracles through Paul, so that even handkerchiefs and aprons that had touched him were taken to the sick, and their illnesses were cured and the evil spirits left them" (Acts 19:11-12).

Can we better understand then, why several years later he wrote to the church that had been planted in that same city of Ephesus, exhorting them:

> "As for you, you were dead in your transgressions and sins, in which you used to live when you followed the ways of this world and of the ruler of the kingdom of the air, the spirit who is now at work in those who are disobedient" (Ephesians 2: 1-2).

> "...and do not give the devil a foothold" (Ephesians 4:27).

> "Have nothing to do with the fruitless deeds of darkness, but rather expose them. For it is shameful even to mention what the disobedient do in secret" (Ephesians 5:11-12).

> "Be very careful, then, how you live – not as unwise but as wise, making the most of every opportunity, because the days are evil" (Ephesians 5:15-16).

◄ PURPOSEFUL EVANGELISM AND MISSIONS

> "Finally, be strong in the Lord and in his mighty power. Put on the full armor of God so that you can take your stand against the devil's schemes.
>
> For our struggle is not against flesh and blood, but against the rulers, against the authorities, against the powers of this dark world and against the spiritual forces of evil in the heavenly realms.
>
> Therefore put on the full armor of God, so that when the day of evil comes, you may be able to stand your ground, and after you have done everything, to stand" (Ephesians 6:10-13).

I wonder if the context within which you minister or the harvest fields to which you carry the gospel are any different, spiritually speaking, from what Paul encountered in his days.

As we read about Paul's experiences in Malta (Acts 28:1-10), we cannot help but see that as the miraculous signs accompanied his ministry (preaching and lifestyle), then people responded more favorably to his message.

If you were to remain unaffected, healthy and strong, after being bitten by a poisonous snake, don't you believe that this would open important ministry doors for you?

As Paul and his team continued to believe God for his promised miraculous signs and wonders, the chief official's father was divinely healed, and "the rest of the sick on the island came and were cured" (Acts 28:9).

It is easy to understand then, why the report states:

> "They honored us in many ways and when we were ready to sail, they furnished us with the supplies needed" (Acts 28:10).

Are people responding favorably to the words which you speak concerning the Kingdom of God? Do they find your message practical, credible, relevant and revolutionary?

What are the signs that have been accompanying your life and ministry, as you share the gospel with the un-evangelized, the un-churched, the backsliders, the religious skeptics, the gospel-hardened cynics and the agnostics of this generation ?

Are you believing God for his supernatural endorsement, or are you still trying to philosophize, intellectualize, and theologize, while your words fall flat, on dry ground?

The days of miracles are not over, and let us be reminded that, as Jesus himself said:

> "According to your faith will it be done to you" (Matthew 9:29).

CHAPTER 8

While You Are Going

"Therefore go and make disciples of all nations, baptizing them in the name of the Father and of the Son and of the Holy Spirit, and teaching them to obey everything I have commanded you. And surely I am with you always, to the very end of the age" (Matthew 28: 19-20).

While structured evangelistic programs, strategies and methods all have their place in our churches, the experiences of the New Testament disciples were primarily based on spontaneous lifestyle evangelism.

They were witnesses of Jesus Christ wherever they went, and the preaching of the gospel was a normal part of their daily activities. They could find an opportunity in every situation, and knew that anytime was a good time to be a witness for the Lord Jesus Christ.

We are reminded of Paul's instruction to young Timothy:

"In the presence of God and of Christ Jesus, who will judge the living and the dead, and in view of his appearing and his kingdom, I give you this charge: Preach the word; be prepared in season and out of season; correct, rebuke and encourage – with great patience and careful instruction" (2 Timothy 4:1-2).

He also encouraged the church in Colosse:

"Be wise in the way you act toward outsiders; make the most of every opportunity. Let your conversation be always full of grace, seasoned with salt, so that you may know how to answer everyone" (Colossians 4:5-6).

Peter also appealed to "God's elect, strangers in the world" to "set apart Christ as Lord" in their hearts, and:

"always be prepared to give an answer to everyone who asks you to give the reason for the hope that you have..." (1 Peter 3:15).

A careful look at Acts 1:8 will reveal that Jesus told his disciples to wait for the power from the Holy Spirit, "and you will be my witnesses in Jerusalem, and in all Judea and Samaria, and to the ends of the earth."

The disciples in the early Church demonstrated that they clearly understood Jesus' will for them to become his 24-7 witnesses, instead of merely going out to witness, occasionally. Their mindset was that of persons who were 100% Christians... 100% of the time.

It was this posture, I believe, that made it easy for Peter to preach up a storm after the healing at Gate Beautiful (Acts 3), even though he had not been able to reach his scheduled prayer meeting, and without even a choir or praise and worship team to back him up.

When, in the middle of the night with tired, bleeding bodies, Paul and Silas needed to lead a troubled jailer to find salvation in Jesus Christ, they were more than ready. They even took time to explain the gospel message to the man's entire household, and subsequently water baptized them...all before the dawn of day. (Acts 16:25-34)

Paul, even though a prisoner in chains (Acts 21:27- 22:21) standing precariously before a trigger-happy Jewish mob, was not too flustered or distracted. He used this opportunity to ask the commander of the soldiers: "May I say something to you? ....Please let me speak to the people" (Acts 21:37, 39).

He then proceeded to share a detailed account of his testimony, pointing his hearers to God's mercy and grace, while serving as a conduit for God's convicting Holy Spirit to work on their hearts.

The early believers seemed like they were willing to identify with their Lord Jesus Christ, at all times and in every kind of situation; whether they were being mocked and criticized (Acts 2:13), unjustly interrogated and beaten (Acts 4-5), stoned to death (Acts 7:54-60, 14:19-20), scattered like wild animals (Acts 8:4), confronted by sorcerers (Acts 8:9-25, 13:6-12), surrounded by philosophers (Acts 17:16-34), in a shipwreck on the open seas (Acts 27:13-44) or under military guard in Caesar's Rome (Acts 28:17-31).

These men and women of God functioned like good spiritual Boy Scouts, always prepared for any eventuality, with a sense of purpose, mission and destiny. They knew that their lives were not their own and that their primary concern was to be ambassadors of Jesus Christ and agents of reconciliation...wherever they were.

Christians, today, especially those of us who live in the Western world have, on the contrary, developed the practice of packaging our lives into neat, convenient, distinct compartments, which are often mutually exclusive.

We, therefore, make a clear-cut demarcation between our spiritual (or religious) lives and our secular lives; giving God a portion and keeping the rest for ourselves.

This means, basically, that we have set times to pray, to worship

God, to read our Bibles, to give to the poor and to share the gospel with the lost. Outside of these prescribed times, we are "off duty" and should not be expected to participate in any of these "religious" activities.

We read in Matthew 28:19,

> "Therefore go and make disciples of all nations, baptizing them in the name of the Father and of the Son and of the Holy Spirit ."

In Mark 16:15, Jesus instructed his disciples:

> "Go into all the world and preach the good news to all creation."

A thorough study of both Matthew 28:19 and Mark 16:15, based on the original Greek words used, will, however, reveal that the literal meaning for the word that is here translated as "go" is ... "going", or "as you are going", or "while you are going".

Jesus, among other things, was instructing them to preach the gospel and make disciples of all nations, while going about their normal, everyday lives... as his witnesses.

His focus was not on special evangelistic programs, strategies or methods, but instead, on lifestyle evangelism, as led by the Holy Spirit.

The logical question that we must ask ourselves is: "How much gospel do we share, while we are going?"

Can we boldly declare that we too are full-time witnesses of Jesus Christ, or do we have to shamefully confess that we are only part-time Christians, reluctantly sharing the gospel when forced to do so by our church leaders or because of adverse circumstances?

Do we see ourselves as bold, courageous ambassadors of Christ or are we more content to serve as carefully disguised, well camouflaged, anonymous secret agents?

As we read through the book of Acts we will notice that

there were no pre-planned "open-air" or "crusade meetings". Evangelistic opportunities came as the disciples faithfully lived their lives, being led by the Holy Spirit.

Their lives were like well-functioning color television sets.

As long as they were switched on and the current was flowing, then the watching world could both see and hear the unadulterated gospel message coming from their innermost beings.

It was obvious that they understood the meaning of that old Evangelical hymn which reminds us:

> "What you are speaks so loud that the world can't hear what you say. They're looking at your walk, not listening to your talk... they're judging from your actions everyday. Don't believe that you'll deceive by claiming what you've never known. They'll accept what they see, and know you to be. They'll judge from your life, alone."

Opportunities for lifestyle evangelism was an everyday affair, and did not have to wait for a special "Outreach Sunday", "Missions Emphasis", "Easter Crusade" or "Annual Church Convention".

Acts 5:42 reminds us that:

> "Day after day, in the temple courts and from house to house, they never stopped teaching and proclaiming the good news that Jesus is the Christ."

Peter and John made it clear in Acts 4:19-20:

> "Judge for yourselves whether it is right in God's sight to obey you rather than God. For we cannot help speaking about what we have seen and heard."

Even when Paul was arrested and being tried before Agrippa and Festus (Acts 26), he took the opportunity to share about Christ.

In verses 27-29 we find:

PURPOSEFUL EVANGELISM AND MISSIONS

"King Agrippa, do you believe the prophets? I know you do."

"Then Agrippa said to Paul, Do you think that in such a short time you can persuade me to become a Christian?"

"Paul replied, Short time or long – I pray God that not only you but all who are listening to me today may become what I am, except for these chains."

These New Testament disciples obviously understood the urgency of their times and the necessity to share the "power of God for the salvation to everyone who believes" (Romans 1:16), with every living human being, regardless of socio-economic status, political pedigree, diplomatic rank or intellectual accomplishments.

The Acts narrative also confirms the strong relationship between prayer-soaked living and spontaneous, supernatural, sustainable evangelistic experiences.

The disciples maintained an ongoing dependence on the Sovereign Lord and were, therefore, able to do some of what they saw their Heavenly Father doing.

Prayer, for them, was not simply a boring, ritualistic exercise that was done out of custom, duty, fear or convenience. Prayer meant, instead, staying energized by God's Holy Spirit, anchored to God's Word and remaining focused on God's purposes...as they kept on going.

How then do we, as *enlightened* 21st century Christians, compare in our own prayer lives? Is the presence of Jesus Christ evident in our daily activities... and are we in close, continuous communication with him?

Are we sharing the Gospel *while we are going*; to work, school, social events, business meetings, on the sports field, at our recreation centers, in our residential communities, over the cell phones, in the highly populated cyberspace and wherever else we go?

What are the Obstacles preventing this from becoming an

everyday reality, in our own lives?

Could it be...blatant sins, fears, doubts, lack of compassion, ignorance of God's Word, haughtiness and pride, Pharisaic religiosity, frustration, insecurity... or possibly... lukewarmness and spiritual insularity?

How then, do we break the back of these counter-productive strongholds and remove these toxic impediments from our lives, so that we might become true ambassadors of Jesus Christ?

Shouldn't we do some honest stock-taking, recommit ourselves to Jesus Christ as His faithful servants, willing to become whatever he wants us to be, and open to be changed in whatever ways necessary?

Isn't it time that we become full-time witnesses, confidently proclaiming the gospel of God's kingdom... while we are going?

CHAPTER 9

All Things To All Men

"To the weak I became weak, to win the weak. I have become all things to all men so that by all possible means I might save some" (1 Corinthians 9:22).

Based on such passages as Matthew 24:14, Matthew 28:19-20, Mark 13:10 and Mark 16:15, the gospel message needs to be communicated to all people, everywhere.

We must learn to effectively share the gospel with all types of people, within their own cultural context, and without causing any unnecessary offense, misunderstanding or confusion.

Since the gospel is (according to Rom. 1:16) the power of God unto salvation, then we have the responsibility to reach as many people as possible, through any means available.

Paul made it clear that he was willing even to die, if necessary, for the sake of the gospel (Acts 20; 22-24, Acts 21:10-11).

The truth is that if a treasure is truly worth living for, then it should also be worth dying for.

Paul further declared to the Church that:

"Though I am free and belong to no man, I make myself a slave to everyone, to win as many as possible" (1 Corinthians 9:19).

PURPOSEFUL EVANGELISM AND MISSIONS

In 1 Corinthians 9:20-22, he continued to explain that, to the Jews he became like a Jew, to those under the law he became like one under the law, to those without law he became like one without law, and to the weak he became weak, all being done to evangelize the lost and to win as many souls as possible.

He had, indeed, become all things to all men so that by all possible means he might save some.

One of the important questions that we must, therefore, ask ourselves is:

"To what extent are we willing to become all things to all men, for the gospel sake?"

Another way we might want to evaluate our own evangelistic quotient is to explore:

"What are some of our personal preferences or cultural practices that we would not readily want to give up, even for the Gospel sake?"

If, for example, as a *liberated Christian woman,* God sends you into a mission field where your pants, jewelry and processed hair are offensive to the non-Christians whom you desire to reach... then what next?

And, what if, before they even listened to your message, they required that you cover your head with a broad yellow hat, a thick ugly scarf or long black veil? Would you take that as God's signal to abandon the mission and return home, or would you be willing to make the adjustments?

If, as in the case of Tanzania (East Africa), you are told that it is offensive or distracting for a man and his wife to be holding hands in public...would you arrogantly defy their traditions, simply to prove an insignificant, counter-productive point?

If, as you carried the gospel, you discovered that bathroom (restroom) and toilet facilities were not the same every where else, as they were back home...What would you do?

How much of our Caribbean or Western mindset are we really willing to give up as we interact with the un-evangelized multitudes from "every tribe and language and people and nation" of this world?

All of us, if we are honest with ourselves, tend to embrace practices and convictions that may easily become eternal stumbling blocks for the un-regenerated, as we attempt to interact with persons of other cultures.

When the wealthy come into our midst, stepping out of their SUV's, all decked out in gold, silver and costly apparel…do we treat then any differently from the poor man in shabby clothes?

Is it possible that you have already decided what kind of nationality or ethnic background your sons-in-law and daughters-in- law should bear…and aren't there some racial groups that you have categorically dismissed as totally unacceptable?

We observe, in Acts 10, that even Peter the anointed apostle, had some serious prejudices, which God had to promptly confront, before sending him into Cornelius' home.

In the story of the "Good Samaritan" (Luke 10:25-37), we note with interest, that it was the despised Samaritan who showed love towards the battered and bruised Jewish man that had fallen into the hands of robbers.

He never allowed the very current Jew vs. Samaritan conflict to prevent him from doing the necessary good to rescue his suffering fellow human being. He became what he needed to be in order to do what he needed to do.

One often wonders what would have been the outcome if the tables had been turned, so that it was the Samaritan who was in need of help. Do you believe that the noble Jewish gentleman would have left his comfort zone to enter dangerous, dirty Samaritan territory?

How do we who bear God's precious seed fit into these stories? How do we relate to the billions of other human beings in this world who don't look, sound, behave and smell like us?

PURPOSEFUL EVANGELISM AND MISSIONS

What are our prejudices? Are they coming in the way of our being able to freely share the gospel... anywhere, and with anyone?

What are some of the adjustments that you would need to make in your life if you were called by God to be his witness in Haiti, India, Afghanistan, Nunavut, Iran, East Africa or Communist China?

How well do you identify with the ...poor, rich, un-educated, intellectual, religious, un-godly, young, old, healthy, sick, popular, un-popular... and all the other non-Christians who you encounter everyday?

Are they able to understand the gospel message which you share? What degree of sacrifices are you willing to make so that their wounds can be bandaged, and the healing oil and wine poured into their lives?

Have we seriously considered the value of rescuing one life from eternal condemnation or the winning of a single soul?

Jesus patiently tried to communicate this to the disciples of his day, in discourses such as the following:

> "Then he said to them all: If anyone would come after me, he must deny himself and take up his cross daily and follow me. For whoever wants to save his life will lose it, but whoever loses his life for me will save it. What good is it for a man to gain the whole world, and yet lose or forfeit his very self?" (Luke 9:23-25)

> "What good will it be for a man if he gains the whole world, yet forfeits his soul? Or what can a man give in exchange for his soul?" (Matthew 16:26)

> "Then he said to them, Watch out! Be on your guard against all kinds of greed; a man's life does not consist in the abundance of his possessions" (Luke 12:15).

> "But God said to him, You fool! This very night your life

will be demanded from you. Then who will get what you have prepared for yourself? This is how it will be with anyone who stores up things for himself but is not rich toward God" (Luke 12:20-21).

"The time came when the beggar died and the angels carried him to Abraham's side. The rich man also died and was buried.

In hell, where he was in torment, he looked up and saw Abraham far away, with Lazarus by his side.

So he called to him, Father Abraham, have pity on me and send Lazarus to dip the tip of his finger in water and cool my tongue, because I am in agony in this fire.

But Abraham replied, Son, remember that in your lifetime you received your good things, while Lazarus received bad things, but now he is comforted here and you are in agony.

And besides all this, between us and you a great chasm has been fixed, so that those who want to go from here to you cannot, nor can anyone cross over from there to us.

He answered, Then I beg you, father, send Lazarus to my father's house, for I have five brothers. Let him warn them, so that they will not also come to this place of torment" (Luke 16:22-28).

In the light of such graphic disclosures, don't you think that there is sufficient urgency for us to willingly become "all things to all men so that by all possible means we might save some"?

If we needed to learn some new languages, or to dress differently or to radically change our diets in order that we might have a platform from which to address the lost, in a particular region of the world...what would be our response?

PURPOSEFUL EVANGELISM AND MISSIONS

How desperately do we want to see lost souls "snatched from the fire" (Jude 1:23) or to see the captives set free (Luke 4:18) and the "worst of sinners" (1 Timothy 1:12-16) saved by God's grace?

Paul once reminded the Church in Corinth of the dreadful judgment from which they had been rescued, and why there now needed to be genuine concern for others who were presently living in sin:

"Do you not know that the wicked will not inherit the kingdom of God?

Do not be deceived: Neither the sexually immoral nor idolaters nor adulterers nor male prostitutes nor homosexual offenders nor thieves nor the greedy nor drunkards nor slanderers nor swindlers will inherit the kingdom of God.

And that is what some of you were. But you were washed, you were sanctified, you were justified in the name of the Lord Jesus Christ and by the Spirit of our God" (1 Corinthians 6:9-11).

What will it take for those of us who now have the assurance of salvation to reach out unto the highways and byways, with the same transforming message of forgiveness of sins, justification, sanctification, regeneration, reconciliation, hope...and more, that are available through receiving the simple gospel of Jesus Christ?

The Teacher (Preacher) confidently declares:

"The fruit of the righteous is a tree of life, and he who wins souls is wise" (Proverbs 11:30).

Daniel further reveals:

"Multitudes who sleep in the dust of the earth will awake; some to everlasting life, others to shame and everlasting contempt.

Those who are wise will shine like the brightness of the heavens, and those who lead many to righteousness, like the stars for ever and ever" (Daniel 12:3).

How willing are you to awaken from your slumber and to militantly step out to "become all things to all men" in order to win souls?

A word to the wise...should be sufficient.

CHAPTER 10

Culture, Customs and Concerns

"The brothers at Lystra and Iconium spoke well of him. Paul wanted to take him along on the journey, so he circumcised him because of the Jews who lived in the area, for they all knew that his father was a Greek" (Acts 16:2-3).

Culture is, according to Paul G. Hiebert:

"The integrated system of learned patterns of behavior, ideas and products characteristic of a society" (p. C9).

"... a people's mental map of their world. It provides them with a guide for their decisions and behavior." (p. C10)

(See: "Perspectives on the World Christian Movement", Revised Edition, 1992, Edited by Ralph D. Winter and Steven C. Hawthorne, William Carey Library, Pasadena, U.S.A.)

As the gospel message is conveyed across geographical barries, we must be careful to avoid causing unnecessary offences that will block the reception to this Good News.

When Paul wanted to take Timothy with him on his missionary journeys (Acts 16:1-5), he made sure that Timothy was circumcised because they did not want to offend the Jews who lived in that region.

We also observe that when Paul and his team entered Jerusalem, they observed some of the Jewish customs:

"The next day Paul took the men and purified himself along with them. Then he went to the temple to give notice of the date when the days of purification would end and the offering would be made for each of them" (Acts 21:26).

The New Testament tells us (1 Timothy 4:3-5, 1 Corinthians 10:25-27), that the Christian is free to eat anything that is set before him, or that is sold in the market place (or meat market) but the same New Testament also warns us that:

"Everything is permissible but not everything is beneficial" (1 Corinthians 10:23).

It is vital, as Christians, that we understand the balance between being free in Christ (Galatians 5:1), on the one hand, and being sensitive, respectful and responsible in our actions, on the other hand, so that you:

"Do not use your freedom to indulge the sinful nature; rather serve one another in love" (Galatians 5:13).

Paul continues, in 1 Corinthians 10:31- 11:1, with the following instructions:

"So whether you eat or drink or whatever you do, do it all for the glory of God. Do not cause anyone to stumble, whether Jews, Greeks or the church of God – even as I try to please everybody in every way. For I am not seeking my own good but the good of many, so that they may be saved. Follow my example, as I follow the example of Christ."

This principle is also reinforced in 1 Corinthians 8:9, where we are warned:

"Be careful, however, that the exercise of your freedom does not become a stumbling block to the weak."

In Romans 14:13, we are further told:

"make up your mind not to put any stumbling block or obstacle in your brother's way."

"If your brother is distressed because of what you eat, you are no longer acting in love. Do not by your eating destroy your brother for whom Christ died" (Romans 14: 15-17).

If the spreading of the gospel, saving of souls and strengthening of believers are our real priorities, then we should:

"make every effort to do what leads to peace and to mutual edification" (Romans 14:19).

Paul concludes that:

"It is better not to eat meat or drink wine or to do anything else that will cause your brother to fall" (Romans 14:21).

The basic principle being taught is that Christians need to be respectful of those around them, sensitive to their culture (customs) and be willing to adjust and adapt where possible.

As we travel with the gospel across different cultures (nations), one of our main aims should be to communicate clearly and effectively with passion, understanding and meaning.

Effective evangelism and missions will only happen as we take time to understand the ministry context, and make the necessary adjustments in our thinking, speaking and doing, as we go with the gospel.

It is also important that we do not make the same mistake as countless other "missionaries", who confused the gospel message with cultural expectations, and, therefore forced those who were receiving the gospel to also embrace non-essential, cultural practices and traditions.

As Peter addressed the first Jerusalem Council, comprising the apostles and elders, he strongly appealed to them:

> "God, who knows the heart, showed that he accepted them by giving the Holy Spirit to them, just as he did to us. He made no distinction between us and them, for he purified their hearts by faith.
>
> Now then, why do you try to test God by putting on the necks of the disciples a yoke that neither we nor our fathers have been able to bear" (Acts 15:10) nor "make it difficult for the Gentiles who are turning to God" (Acts 15:19).

As we preach the gospel, we must ensure that we do not major on the minor, or minor on the major; keeping in mind that the essentials of the gospel are:

> "that Christ died for our sins according to the Scriptures, that he was buried, and that he was raised on the third day according to the Scriptures" (1 Corinthians 15:3-4).

The true disciple of Jesus Christ must, therefore, keep his focus on the kernel of the gospel and not allow himself to become a slave of any particular culture, whether his own or that of the nations to be reached.

While displaying the necessary respect and observing the required protocols, the ambassador of Jesus Christ needs to be flexible as he crosses over geographical zones and cultural hurdles.

Jesus, himself, displayed his regard for Jewish culture on several occasions, as indicated by the following accounts:

> He taught publicly in their temple and in their synagogues (Matthew 4:23, Luke 4:44, 13:10, 19:47-48, John 7:14, 26, 28, 37).

CULTURE, CUSTOMS AND CONCERNS ▸

He observed their Jewish Sabbaths (Luke 4:31, 13:10).

He participated in their annual Feasts (Luke 22:7-16, John 2:23, 5:1, 7:14, 11:55-57).

He endorsed their Mosaic Law (Matthew 5:17-20, Luke 16:16-17).

He gave respect to their Priests (Matthew 7:4, Luke 17:12-14).

He affirmed them as God's Israel (Matthew 10:57, 15:24-26).

He paid his temple taxes as was required (Matthew 17:24-27, 22:15-22).

Jesus also demonstrated, in no uncertain way, that neither his disciples nor himself were to become trapped by any social, religious or cultural expectations, as illustrated in the following scenes:

Jesus confronted their slavery to the Sabbath (Matthew 12:1-14, Mark 2:23-28, Luke 6:1-11, 13:10-17, 14:1-6, John 9:13-16).

He challenged the Traditions of the Elders (Matthew 15:1-20, 16:5-12, 21:43-4, 23:1-39, Mark 7:1-23).

He reinterpreted the Mosaic Law (Matthew 5:21-48, 19:1-12).

He disregarded their Social Prejudices (Matthew 15:21-28, Mark 1:40-42, 2:13-17, 7:24-30, 10:13-18, 46-52, 14:1-11, Luke 7:36-50, 18:15-17, 19:1-10, John 4:4-26, 8:1-11).

He redefined their meaning of Worship (John 4:19-24).

◄ PURPOSEFUL EVANGELISM AND MISSIONS

His ministry superseded that of the Teachers of the Law (Matthew 4:23-25, 9:1-8, 27-34, 22:33, Mark 1:27-34, Mark 2:12, 4:39-41, 5:1-20, 7:36-37, Luke 7:11-17, 13:17, 45-46, John 3:1-21).

There is a place for cultural awareness and affirmation as we spread the gospel, but this should always be balanced off by Spiritual sensitivity and discernment, as we keep our focus on the greater purposes of God for his people.

Success in cross-cultural missions will become more attainable when we realize that the life-changing gospel that we carry is not culture-bound, but transcends all customs, systems and religious traditions.

In the midst of all our going, doing and being, we cannot afford to ignore the central role which prayer and intersession must play in the lives of authentic servants of Jesus Christ.

Evangelism, missions and discipleship-making are all Spirit-directed enterprises, which require submission to God's will and dependence on his power, wisdom and grace.

Paul, even though considered a stalwart apostle and miracle-worker, was careful to make the following requests as he traversed land and sea with the gospel message:

> "And pray in the Spirit on all occasions with all kinds of prayers and requests. With this in mind, be alert and always keep on praying for all the saints.
>
> Pray also for me, that whenever I open my mouth, words may be given me so that I will fearlessly make known the mystery of the gospel, for which I am an ambassador in chains.
>
> Pray that I may declare it fearlessly, as I should" (Ephesians 6:18-20).

CULTURE, CUSTOMS AND CONCERNS

"Brothers, pray for us" (1 Thessalonians 5:25).

He also made it clear that a significant portion of his own ministry was taken up in praying for fellow Christians in the various regions:

"I always thank God for you because of his grace given you in Christ Jesus" (1 Corinthians 1:4).

"For this reason, ever since I heard about your faith in the Lord Jesus and your love for all the saints, I have not stopped giving thanks for you , remembering you in my prayers.

I keep asking that the God of our Lord Jesus Christ, the glorious Father, may give you the Spirit of wisdom and revelation, so that you may know him better.

I pray also that the eyes of your heart may be enlightened in order that you may know the hope to which he has called you, the riches of his glorious inheritance in the saints, and his incomparably great power for us who believe..." (Ephesians 1:15-19).

"I thank my God every time I remember you. In all my prayers for all of you. I always pray with joy because of your partnership in the gospel from the first day until now, being confident of this, that he who began a good work in you will carry it on to completion until the day of Christ Jesus" (Philippians 1:3-6).

"And this is my prayer; that your love may abound more and more in knowledge and depth of insight, so that you may be able to discern what is best and may be pure and blameless until the day of Christ, filled with the fruit of righteousness that comes through Jesus Christ – to the glory and praise of God" (Philippians 1:9-11).

PURPOSEFUL EVANGELISM AND MISSIONS

"We always thank God, the Father of our Lord Jesus Christ, when we pray for you…" (Colossians 1:3).

"For this reason, since the day we heard about you, we have not stopped praying for you and asking God to fill you with the knowledge of his will through all spiritual wisdom and understanding.

And we pray this in order that you may live a life worthy of the Lord and may please him in every way…" (Colossians 1:9-10).

"We always thank God for all of you, mentioning you in our prayers. We continually remember before our God and Father your work produced by faith, your labor prompted by love, and your endurance inspired by hope in our Lord Jesus Christ" (1 Thessalonians 1:2-3).

"With this in mind, we constantly pray for you, that our God may count you worthy of his calling…We pray this so that the name of our Lord Jesus may be glorified in you, and you in him, according to the grace of our God and the Lord Jesus Christ" (2 Thessalonians 1:11-12).

"I thank God, whom I serve, as my forefathers did, with a clear conscience, as night and day I constantly remember you in my prayers" (2 Timothy 1:3).

"I always thank my God as I remember you in my prayers, because I hear about your faith in the Lord Jesus and your love for all the saints. I pray that you may be active in sharing your faith, so that you will have a full understanding of every good thing we have in Christ" (Philemon 1:4-6).

An active, vibrant and intensifying prayer life will help to ensure that witnesses of Jesus Christ maintain their evangelistic focus, develop in Christian character, imbibe Godly wisdom, overflow with

Spiritual power and abound in unconditional love.

The critical need for all these qualities will be most clearly appreciated when one is called to minister across cultural boundaries, where circumstances are never static, human understanding always limited and physical safety is never guaranteed.

All who feel, sense, hear or know God's calling on their lives to serve in his vast harvest field will need to prepare well. Let us also endeavor to pray even more militantly than ever, because these are definitely difficult, challenging, unpredictable and evil days.

Conclusion

Woe Is Me If I Preach Not The Gospel

As we seriously contemplate the Great Commission, to "make disciples of all nations", it becomes obvious that:

The whole world is in need of the Gospel message.

Without the salvation that comes through a personal relationship with Jesus Christ, all human beings will be eternally lost.

Those who already know him have the responsibility to make him known to the rest of the world.

We who refuse to "make disciples" must ultimately give an account to Almighty God.

The following story has often been told with a variety of modifications, but with the same essential point. I trust that you also will appreciate its message.

There was once a blind man who was accustomed to making his daily trips from home to work and back, along a well trodden route. This took him across a narrow wooden bridge, overlooking a very deep ravine.

One Thursday, during the early afternoon, a powerful freak storm suddenly eroded the foundations and washed away the once faithful bridge.

PURPOSEFUL EVANGELISM AND MISSIONS

As the uninformed blind man approached the water-soaked roadway on his after-work journey home, Mr. Blowhard, his God-fearing neighbor was reclining on his verandah and remarked to himself: "Someone ought to tell that blind man that the bridge has been washed away".

After a few more minutes, as the blind man approached the spot where the bridge used to be, the very concerned Mr. Blowhard spoke again: "You know...I am convinced that somebody really should tell that blind man about the danger; that the bridge is no longer there" ...and he returned to reading the sports page in his newspaper.

As the blind man made his final step, plunging into an unexpected eternity, Mr. Blowhard again raised up his troubled eyes from his afternoon papers, shook his head in anger and shouted on the top of his voice: "See! I told you! ...Someone should have told that poor, blind man that the bridge had been washed away!"

How do we who claim to be the light of the world, the salt of the earth, the Lord's witnesses and the select ambassadors of Jesus Christ, relate to the spiritual blindness in this present generation?

Will we continue to sit at ease in Zion (like Mr. Blowhard), watch the multitudes perish around us everyday and blame everyone else for their destruction, or are we prepared to step in and sound the alarm?

Ezekiel records for us the following instructions from the Sovereign Lord:

"Son of man, I have made you a watchman for the house of Israel; so hear the word I speak and give them warning from me. When I say to the wicked, 'O wicked man, you will surely die,' and you do not speak out to dissuade him from his ways, that wicked man will die for his sin, and I will hold you accountable for his blood. But if you do warn the wicked man to turn from his ways and he does not do so, he will die for his sin, but you will have saved yourself" (Ezekiel 33:7-9).

How would you respond if you saw that your neighbor's house were on fire, while he and his entire family were fast asleep on the inside?

Would you reason that since you know they needed their night's rest then you wouldn't bother to disturb them, or that it would be too embarrassing for the crowds that were already gathering outside… to see them in their multi-colored pajamas?

Would you allow them to sleep off into an extremely hot eternity or would you take some responsibility to alert them of the impending destruction, and give them an opportunity to make their own decisions?

Wasn't it the New Testament writer, Jude, who exhorted us:

"Be merciful to those who doubt; snatch others from the fire and save them; to others show mercy, mixed with fear – hating even the clothing stained by corrupted flesh" (Jude 1:22-23).

We are reminded of a run-away prophet by the name of Jonah, who was eagerly anticipating the destruction of an entire city of people who were so confused and spiritually blind, that they could not even "tell their right hand from their left" (Jonah 4:11).

We, like Jonah, know the established fact that our Lord is "a gracious and compassionate God, slow to anger and abounding in love, a God who relents from sending calamity" (Jonah 4:2).

Shouldn't we, therefore, in contrast to Jonah's actions, grab at every opportunity to proclaim the life-transforming gospel, so that those who are lost may be redeemed by the blood of the Lamb, completely reconciled to the Father and regenerated by the power of his Holy Spirit?

We certainly have not been rescued by Almighty God, simply to lie down in green pastures and drink our belly full from the still waters, without being genuinely concerned for those who are continuously being mauled by the lions and bears in the dark, arid, lonely places.

It is essential, if we claim to be followers of Jesus Christ, that we develop the same love and compassion as he had for the "harassed and helpless" who were "like sheep without a shepherd" (Matthew 9:36), and for whom more workers are desperately needed.

The Bible, using another metaphor, pictures the authentic Christian as a branch, fruit tree or vineyard that is expected to reproduce good fruit, after its own kind.

The writer in John 15, after establishing that the believer is likened to a branch, extending from the True Vine ... goes on to appeal for the bearing of fruit (v.2), more fruit (v.2), much fruit (v.8) and fruit that will remain (v.8).

One way in which this fruit should manifest itself is through the deliberate winning and discipling of souls, as indicated in the following Scripture portions:

"The fruit of the righteous is a tree of life, and he who wins souls is wise" (Proverbs 11:30).

"Those who are wise will shine like the brightness of the heavens, and those who lead many to righteousness, like the stars for ever and ever" (Daniel 12:3).

"Go into all the world and preach the good news to all creation" (Mark 16:15).

"Therefore go and make disciples of all nations, baptizing them in the name of the Father and of the Son and of the Holy Spirit, and teaching them to obey everything I have commanded you" (Matthew 28:19-20).

"Preach the Word; be prepared in season and out of season; correct, rebuke and encourage – with great

CONCLUSION

patience and careful instruction ... do the work of an evangelist, discharge all the duties of your ministry" (2 Timothy 4:2-5).

"And the things you have heard me say in the presence of many witnesses entrust to reliable men who will also be qualified to teach others" (2 Timothy 2:2).

"Then he told this parable: 'A man had a fig tree, planted in his vineyard, and he went to look for fruit on it, but did not find any. So he said to the man who took care of the vineyard. For three years now I've been coming to look for fruit on this fig tree and haven't found any. Cut it down! Why should it use up the soil?

Sir, the man replied, leave it alone for one more year, and I'll dig around it and fertilize it. If it bears fruit next year, fine! If not, then cut it down'" (Luke 13:6-9).

Please note that the unproductive branch or tree was to be "cut down" and thrown away, while the ones which produced fruit would be encouraged to produce much more.

In Jesus' own words:

"This is my Father's glory, that you bear much fruit, showing yourselves to be my disciples...You did not choose me, but I chose you and appointed you to go and bear fruit—fruit that will last" (John 15:8, 16).

None of us knows for certain how many more fruit-bearing years we have on this earth, at what time Jesus will return to judge the living and the dead or when death will come knocking at our doors.

James raised the disturbing, but necessary, question:

"Now listen, you who say, 'Today or tomorrow we will go to this or that city, spend a year there, carry on business and make money'. Why, you do not even know what will happen tomorrow. What is your life? You are a mist that appears for a little while and then vanishes" (James 4:13-14).

The writer in the Proverbs also issues a clear warning:

"Do not boast about tomorrow, for you do not know what a day may bring forth" (Proverbs 27:1).

In light of these cautions, Jesus' clear words regarding his own ministry-posture, come into even greater focus:

"As long as it is day, we must do the work of him who sent me. Night is coming, when no one can work. While I am in the world, I am the light of the world" (John 9:4-5).

We, as his faithful disciples, are likewise called to reach the lost and perishing, with a motivating sense of urgency, not knowing for sure when our night will come.

Paul, within this context, also pleads with the believer:

"For we must all appear before the judgment seat of Christ, that each one may receive what is due him for the things done while in the body, whether good or bad" (2 Corinthians 5:10).

"Since, then, we know what it is to fear the Lord, we try to persuade men..." (2 Corinthians 5:11)

"For Christ's love compels us, because we are convinced that one died for all, and therefore all died. And he died for all, that those who live should no longer live for themselves but for him who died for them and was raised again" (2 Corinthians 5:14-15).

"All this is from God who reconciled us to himself through Christ and gave us the ministry of reconciliation...and he has committed to us the message of reconciliation" (2 Corinthians 5:18-19).

"We are therefore Christ's ambassadors, as though God were making his appeal through us. We implore you on Christ's behalf: Be reconciled to God" (2 Corinthians 5:20).

As we live out our Christian lives, on a daily basis, whether as platform ministers or lifestyle evangelists, we have a clear mandate from God to proclaim the Gospel; evangelizing the lost and discipling the converted.

I might be an excellent administrator, a gifted musician, an eloquent orator, an anointed miracle worker, or a faithful, reliable, helpful church member, but: "Woe to me if I do not preach the gospel" (1 Corinthians 9:16).

APPENDIX 1

CONSIDERATIONS FOR CULTURE AND EVANGELISM / MISSIONS

{Quotes taken from "Perspectives on the World Christian Movement", Revised Edition, 1992, Edited by Ralph D. Winter and Steven C. Hawthorne, Published by William Carey Library, Pasadena, California, U.S.A.}

What is Culture?

"Culture is a very inclusive word. It takes into account linguistic, political, economic, social, psychological, religious, national, racial, and other differences." (David J. Hesselgrave, p. C35)

"Culture is a way of thinking, feeling, believing. It is the group's knowledge stored up for future use." (Clyde Kluckhohn, p.C35)

"Culture is a design for living. It is a plan according to which society adapts itself to its physical, social, and ideational environment." (Louis Luzbetak, p.C35)

Culture is; "The integrated system of learned patterns of behaviour, ideas and products characteristic of a society." (Paul G. Hiebert, p.C9)

"A culture is a people's mental map of their world. It provides them with a guide for their decisions and behavior." (Paul G. Hiebert, p.C10)

N.B. "The most basic procedure in a study of culture is to become a master of one's own. Everyone has a culture. No one can ever divorce himself from his culture"." (Lloyd E. Kwast, p.C3)

Some Illustrations Of Cultural Differences

1. One cannot say to the Zanaki people along the winding shores of sprawling Lake Victoria, "Behold, I stand at the door and knock" (Rev.3:20). This would mean that Christ was declaring Himself to be a thief, for in Zanakli land thieves generally make it a practice to knock on the door of a hut which they hope to burglarize, and if they hear any movement or noise inside, they dash off into the dark. An honest man will come to a house and call the name of the person inside, and this way identify himself by his voice. Accordingly, in the Zanaki translation it is necessary to say, "Behold I stand at the door and call". (David J. Hesselgrave, p.C39)
2. To understand a strange culture one must enter as much as possible into the very life and viewpoint of the native people. Otherwise, a person will not realize how ridiculous it is to talk to Indians of southern Mexico about **scribes who "devour widows' houses" (Mark 12:40)**. Their houses are often made with cornstalk walls and grass roofs, and farm animals do eat them when fodder gets scarce, so that people guard against hungry cows breaking in to eat down

a house. "Devouring widows' houses" is no bold metaphor in some places, but a real danger. Hence the native reader wonders; **"What were these 'scribes' anyway? Was this just a name for starved, ravenous cattle?"** In such cases one must translate "destroy widows' houses". (David J. Hesselgrave, p.C39)
3. We begin learning about a culture by observing the behavior of the people and looking for patterns in the behavior. For example, we have all seen two **American men on meeting grasp each other's hand and shake it. In Mexico we would see them embrace. In India each puts his hands together and raises them towards his forehead with a slight bow of the head**—a gesture of greeting that is efficient, for it permits a person to greet a great many others in a simple motion, and clean, for people need not touch each other. The latter is particularly important in a society where the touch of **an untouchable** used to defile **a high caste** person, and force him to take a purification bath. Among the Siriano of South America, **men spit on each other's chests in greeting**. (Paul G. Hiebert, p. C10)
4. On leaving the jungle on a small plane with the local native chief, he (Dr. Jacob Loewen) noticed the chief go to all his fellow tribesmen and **suck their mouths**...The chief explained that **they had learned this custom from the white man**. They had seen that **every time he went up in his plane, he sucked the mouths of his people as magic to insure a safe journey**. Like most cultural patterns, kissing is not a universal human custom. It was absent among most primitive tribesmen, and considered vulgar and revolting to the Chinese who thought it too suggestive of cannibalism. (Hiebert, p.C10)
5. In the airport, at three in the morning, the American traveler is draped uncomfortably over a chair rather than

stretched out on the rug. **He would rather be dignified than comfortable.**

Behind all these behavior patterns is a basic assumption (in American culture) that the ground and floor are dirty. This explains their obsession for getting off the floor. It also explains why they keep their shoes on when they enter the house, and why the mother scolds the child when it picks a potato chip off the floor and eats it. **The floor is "dirty"** even though it has just been washed, and the instant a piece of food touches it, the food becomes dirty.

On the other hand, in Japan the people believe **the floor is clean**. Therefore they take their shoes off at the door, and sleep and sit on mats on the floor. When we walk into their home with our shoes on, they feel much like we do when someone walks on our couch with their shoes on. (Hiebert, p. C11-12)

6. In parts of Arabia, the people have a different concept or map of time. If the meeting time is ten o'clock, only a servant shows up at ten—in obedience to his master. The proper time for others is from ten forty-five to eleven fifteen, just long enough after the set time to show their independence and equality. The problem arises when an American meets an Arab and arranges a meeting for ten o'clock. The American shows up at ten, the "right time" according to him. The Arab shows up at ten forty-five, the "right time" according to him. The American feels the Arab has no sense of time at all (which is false), and the Arab is tempted to think Americans act like servants, which is also false. (Hiebert, p.C12)

North Americans generally stand about four or five feet apart when they discuss general matters. On the other hand, when they want to discuss personal matters, they move in to about two or three feet apart in ordinary conversations and even closer for personal discussions. Misunderstandings arise only when a North American meets a Latin American. The latter subconsciously moves in to about three feet. The former is vaguely uneasy about this and steps back. Now the Latin American feels like he is talking to someone across the room, and so he steps closer. Now the North American is again confused. According to his spacial distance, the Latin American should be discussing personal matters, like sharing some gossip or arranging a bank robbery. But, in fact, he is talking about public matters, about the weather and politics. **The result is the North American thinks that Latin Americans are pushy and always under their nose; the Latin American concludes that North Americans are always distant and cold. (Hiebert, p. C15)**

7. Most Americans shudder when they enter an Indian restaurant and **see the people eating curry and rice with their fingers**. A number of Americans went to a restaurant with an Indian guest, and someone asked the inevitable question, "Do people in India really eat with their fingers?"
"Yes we do," the Indian replied, "but we look at it differently. **You see, we wash our hands carefully, and besides, they have never been in anyone else's mouth. But look at these spoons and forks, and think about how many other people have already had them inside their mouths!**" (Hiebert, p. C16)

8. Some missionaries in Zaire had trouble in building rapport with the people. Finally, one old man explained the people's hesitancy to befriend the missionaries. **"When you came, you brought your strange ways,"** he said. "You brought tins of food. On the outside of one was a picture of a corn. When you opened it inside was corn and you ate it. Outside another was a picture of meat, and inside was meat, and you ate it. **And when you had your baby, you brought small tins. On the outside was**

a picture of babies, and you opened it and fed the inside to your child." (Hiebert, p. C15)

N.B. Misunderstandings are based on **ignorance about another culture**. There is a problem of knowledge. The solution is to **learn to know how the other culture works**. Our first task in entering a new culture is to **be a student** of its ways. Even later, whenever something seems to be going wrong, **we must assume that the people's behavior makes sense to them**, and reanalyze our own understandings of their culture. (Hiebert, p. C15-16)

Before we hastily condemn the cultural practices of other people, consider the following features in **our own culture**:

1. We love to see the **beautiful brides-maids at our wedding ceremonies**, but, did we know that this practice was "**originally used by our non-Christian ancestors to confuse the demons whom, they thought, had come to carry off the bride**"? (Hiebert, p. C21)

2. Why is it we teach, **based on good manners**, that when we have a cold or flu, we should **cough and sneeze in a handkerchief, so that we can store up all that comes out, and keep it in our pockets**?

3. Why is it that in a (hot) tropical region such as ours, we continue to **insist that to be properly dressed for church, a man must wear a jacket and tie?**

4. Why do we (in a poor, developing country) continue to **spend untold millions of dollars annually, burying dead bodies in expensive, elaborate coffins, while thousands of living human beings in our midst, remain homeless?**

5. Why do we speak to each other in normal everyday English and Patois (pronounced *patwa*), but **when we are to speak to God** (in prayer), **we resort to King James English, or a false, accented, religious tone?**

6. Why do we spend millions of dollars building **sanctuaries,**

which normally remain closed**, except for Sundays (or Saturdays) and a few evenings/nights per week?
7. Why do we keep responding; **"fine"**, whenever people ask us; **"How you doing?"** and why do we say; **"yes"**, when they ask; **"Everything O.K.?"** or **"All's well?"**... knowing quite well that we are loaded with tons of problems? And what do we make of the slogan: **"Jamaica, No Problem"**...in light of the escalating economic, social, moral and spiritual crises?

Think on these things.(dksplcccaugust2009)

APPENDIX 2

PORTMORE LANE COVENANT COMMUNITY CHURCH
T2525 Evangelism Outline
(Adapted from Evangelism Explosion International III)

T ……..TESTIMONY

a) Issue:
_____

b) Negative Illustration:
_____

c) Then one day I
_____

d) Since then
_____

e) Positive Illustration:
_____

f) Not only that, but now I know for sure that if
_____

2 DIAGNOSTIC QUESTIONS

I. Have you come to that place in
_____
_____
_____
_____
_____

PURPOSEFUL EVANGELISM AND MISSIONS

II. If you were to die right now and you stood before Almighty God, and he asked you: "Why
_____
_____
?" or
_____
_____
?" What would your answer be?

5 POINTS OF THE GOSPEL

I. **GRACE**: Heaven (or eternal life)
_____
_____

   Scriptures:
   _____
   _____

   Illustrations:
   _____
   _____

   Link:
   _____
   _____

II. **MAN**: Man is
_____
_____

   Scriptures:
   _____
   _____

APPENDIX 2

Illustrations:
_____
_____

Link:
_____
_____

III. **GOD**: God is
_____

but God is also
_____

Scriptures:
_____
_____

Illustrations:
_____
_____

Link:
_____
_____

IV. **CHRIST**: Jesus Christ
_____
_____

Scriptures:
_____
_____

PURPOSEFUL EVANGELISM AND MISSIONS

Illustrations:
_____
_____

Link:
_____
_____

V. FAITH:
_____
_____

Scriptures:
_____
_____

Illustrations:
_____
_____

Link:
_____
_____

2 Follow–Up Questions
a) Does this
_____

b) Would you like to receive
_____

APPENDIX 2

5 Follow Up Steps

a) Bible

b) Prayer

c) Worship

d) Fellowship

e) Witness

The above outline is a modification of what had been originally developed by Dr. D. James Kennedy (Former Pastor of Coral Ridge Presbyterian Church, Fort Lauderdale, Florida, U.S.A.) for the Evangelism Explosion III Ministry. We encourage you to do the complete E.E. training program with a certified Teacher-Trainer.

A completed sample outline is shown below:

T ....Testimony

a) **Issue**: I had a serious problem with being afraid of people, because of deep-rooted insecurity.
b) **Negative Illustration**: I would hide from even my cousins when they came to visit, and refused to play with them. This pattern continued up to my early adult years.
c) **Then one day** I made a decision and received eternal life.
d) **Since then**, I have been able to relate to people in a normal way. I no longer feel afraid or intimidated by anyone.
e) **Positive Illustration**: I now even speak in public a lot and am able to easily introduce myself to people whom I am meeting for the first time.
f) **Not only that**, but now I know for sure that even if I were to die right now, I would have eternal life (or I know for sure that I

PURPOSEFUL EVANGELISM AND MISSIONS

would be going to heaven)...May I ask you a question?

2 Diagnostic Questions

I. **Have you come** to that place in your own life where you know for sure that if you were to die right now, you would have eternal life (or you would be going to heaven)?

{You can know for sure...1 John 5:11-13, John 6:47. May I share with you how I came to know, and how you can know too? But first, may I ask you another question?}

II. **If you were to die** right now and you stood before Almighty God, and he asked you, "Why should I let you spend eternity with me?" or "Why should I let you into my heaven?" What would your answer be?

{Many people believe just the same thing you do, but the surprising thing is that the Bible reveals that:... }

5 Points Of The Gospel

I. **GRACE**: Heaven (or eternal life) is a free gift. It is not earned, deserved ...or to be purchased.
Scriptures: Rom. 6:23, Eph. 2:8-9, Titus 3:5
Illustrations: A birthday gift (already paid for by someone else, being given freely)
Link: The same Bible goes on to tell us that...

II. **MAN**: Man is a sinner and he cannot save himself.
Scriptures: Romans 3:10, Romans 3:23, Isaiah 53:6
Illustrations: *A drowning man cannot save himself or A spoilt orange in the orange juice.*
Link: From the Bible, we also discover that...

III. **GOD**: God is loving and merciful, and wants to forgive us but God is also just and must punish sin.

Scriptures: Exodus 34:7-8, 1 John 4:7-8, Jer. 31:3, Psalm 103:8, Heb. 10:31
Illustrations: A good friend of yours who has become a judge, and whom now faces you in court, knowing that you are guilty of the offense for which you have been charged.
Link: God seemed to have a problem, but he solved this by sending Jesus Christ his Son.

IV. **CHRIST**: Jesus Christ, God's Son (and also God the Son) came and died in our place. He paid the penalty for our sins, and now offers eternal life to us as a free gift.
Scriptures: 2 Cor. 5:21, John 3:16, Isaiah 53:6
Illustrations: An expensive gift, already paid for, and being offered to you freely.
Link: The question that you might be asking right now is "How then, does one receive this gift of eternal life?" ...This gift is received by faith.

V. **FAITH**: Faith is the key that unlocks the door to eternal life. This faith for salvation is not just the same as head belief (James 2:19). This faith is one that produces commitment. It is transferring your trust from your self (or your good works) and trusting in Jesus Christ, alone, for your salvation.
Scriptures: Acts 16:30-31, John 3:16, Acts 4:12, Eph 2:8-9
Illustrations: The bunch of keys or transferring your body weight from your own legs to a chair.
Link: The 2 follow-up Questions

2 Follow—Up Questions

a) Does this make sense to you?
b) Would you like to receive this gift of Eternal Life, right now?
   {If answer is yes, proceed to a simple prayer of repentance/confession/acceptance. See Appendix 3.
   Then explain (to the new convert) the Follow Up Steps (Steps to Growth) below:}

5 Follow Up Steps

a) **Bible** ...Read it on a daily basis. {Provide a reading plan, or make recommendations}

b) **Prayer** ...Pray on a daily basis to keep the conversation going with God.

c) **Worship** ...Suggest a good, progressive Bible-believing Christian Church (possibly your own).

d) **Fellowship**...Encourage the new convert to build satisfying, meaningful relationships with other Christians. {As iron sharpens iron, so one man sharpens another...Prov. 27:17}

e) **Witness**...Share with others about the decision you just made, what Jesus Christ did (and is presently doing) for you, and how others may also have this eternal life.

APPENDIX 3

SALVATION IS FOR ALL, INCLUDING YOU.

You may be a very good person, even like Cornelius, who prayed often, took care of poor people and was a moral, upright man, but, even he, still needed to humbly accept Jesus Christ as his personal Saviour and Lord (Acts 10:1-48).

You may be a very bad person, like Paul, who blasphemed against God, murdered people, and was "the worst of sinners", yet God saved him and turned his life around (1 Tim.1:12-16).

Remember; "If we say we have no sins, the truth is not in us, but if we confess our sins, he is faithful and just to forgive us of our sins and to cleanse us from all unrighteousness" (1 John 1:8-9).

God has provided salvation for all, through Jesus Christ, but you have the freedom of choice to accept or reject. Your own decision will determine your own future, therefore, make the right choice.

Simple Prayer Of Acceptance

Dear God, Creator and Father, I come to you recognizing that I am a sinner and in desperate need of your salvation.

> I know that I cannot save myself, so I humbly place my life before you, asking for your forgiveness and salvation.

PURPOSEFUL EVANGELISM AND MISSIONS

I know that Jesus Christ died in my place so that I might be born again by his Spirit.

I now receive Jesus Christ as my personal Saviour and Lord of my life, and commit my eternity into your hands.

What Next?

Having made the decision to surrender to Jesus Christ as your personal Saviour and Lord, here are some suggestions to ensure purposeful, spiritual growth:

1. Thanksgiving.....Express your sincere gratitude to Almighty God for rescuing you from the eternity described in Luke 16:22-28, Mark 9:42-48 and Rev. 20:11-15
2. Prayer......Keep your focus on Jesus Christ and dependence on him through continuous, daily prayer, as indicated in Prov. 3:5-6, Luke 18:1, 1 Thes. 5:17 and Eph. 6:18.
3. Bible........Read it daily, meditate on it, study it systematically, believe it and obey its teachings (Josh. 1:6-9, Psalm 1, Psalm 119:9-11, 97-105, Acts 17:10-11, 2 Tim. 2:15, 2 Tim.3:16-17, Heb.4:12).
4. Water Baptism......Seek as early as possible to be Water Baptized, as an identification with Jesus Christ, in response to his example and instructions. (Matt. 3:13-17, Rom. 6:1-4, Matt. 28:18-20, Mark 16:15-16, Acts 2:36-41, Acts 8:34-39, Acts 10:47-48)
5. Baptism in The Holy Spirit.....Ask God to baptize (fill or empower) you with his Holy Spirit, so that you may live with the same spiritual power as the early disciples did (Luke 11:9-13, John 7:37-39, Acts 1:4-8, Acts 2:1-21, Acts 8:4-8, Acts 9:15-19, Acts 10:44-48, Acts 19:1-7, Luke 10:19, Mark 16:17-20, 1 Cor.2:1-5).
6. Fellowship.........Bearing in mind that "as iron sharpens iron, so one man sharpens another"(Prov. 27:17), seek

APPENDIX 3

to develop Christian friendships and participate in godly activities (Acts 2:42, Psalm1, Hebrews 10:24-25, 1 Cor.15:33).

7. Local Church.....Submit yourself to a local church and its leadership, so that you will have spiritual covering and accountability for your life, in a setting where there is sound doctrine, caring pastors, Spirit-led worship experiences and sufficient opportunities to give and serve (Acts 2:42-47, Hebrews 13:17, 1 Cor. 12:1-31, Eph. 4:1-16, Rom. 12:1-21).

8. Witness......Share with others what the Lord Jesus Christ has done, and is presently doing, in your life. Let your friends, colleagues and family members know about the decision you have made to live for him, and how they too can be saved. (Acts 1:8, Mark 5: 18-20, John 4:28-30, 1 Tim.1:12-17, Acts 22:6-21, 26:1-29, Rom. 1:16-17, Rom. 10:9-10, Acts 16:30-31, Matt. 28:18-20, Mark 16: 15-16)

Date of Commitment: _____

Signed: _____

www.ingramcontent.com/pod-product-compliance
Lightning Source LLC
LaVergne TN
LVHW091600060526
838200LV00036B/928